THE BLACKBOARD FUMBLE

The Christianity Today Series:

The Sexual Christian, by Tim Stafford

Tough Questions Christians Ask, David Neff, editor

The Blackboard Fumble, Ken Sidey, editor

What Every Christian Should Know,
by Jo H. Lewis and Gordon A. Palmer

THE
BLACKBOARD
FUMBLE

EDITED BY
KEN SIDEY

VICTOR BOOKS ®
A DIVISION OF SCRIPTURE PRESS PUBLICATIONS INC.
USA CANADA ENGLAND

Recommended Dewey Decimal Classification: 371.01
Suggested Subject Heading: MORAL EDUCATION

Library of Congress Catalog Card Number: 89-60148
ISBN: 0-89693-708-9

Cover Illustration: Tim Jonke

CONTENTS

A Question of Values

Ken Sidey

Welcome Class of 2002." The banner hanging at the front of the crowded multipurpose room shocked me into the reality of a new stage of parenthood. My wife and I were attending the kindergarten "roundup" for our oldest child—our first to start school—and suddenly we were facing the next century, with twelve of the most important years of our little girl's life on the line.

I am sure our concerns were much the same as those of the other three hundred or so parents who jammed into that room. We were looking for a "good education" for our child: an education that provides all the information she will need to prosper in our culture, go to college, get a good job; an education that develops in her the ability to think and the curiosity to learn.

But as Christians we brought to that meeting an additional concern, one that is certainly not the exclusive property of believers, but one that especially troubles Christians as they regard the state of public education today. We were concerned not only for the academic content offered in the school, but also for the values taught and promoted there. Would they be consistent with the values we hold? Or would they be at odds? Would our child be indoctrinated? Or would she drift through a moral vacuum?

Our parents, it seems, did not face such questions. Perhaps it was the fifties, or small-town life, but the moral values of my own education seemed stable and clear. The parents of the class of 2002 have no such assurance. Times have changed. And the pointed comment of one parent I spoke with echoes the fear of many Christians as they look at public education today: "How do I know this school isn't going to undermine every value I'm teaching my kids at home and at church?"

The problems of public education are high on the national consciousness: low test scores; high dropout rates; illiteracy; lack of discipline. They form a well-known litany of shortcomings. Little else needs to be written documenting the problems. What is needed is progress toward solutions.

Unfortunately, the Christian press abounds with polemics against public education. Some writers go so far as to declare that public schools have crossed the line of redemption in terms of moral and ethical values. They propose that the only prudent response for Christian parents is to pull their children out of the public schools. Such an argument not only slights the redemptive reach of God's hand, it also ignores Christ's command to be "salt and light" in our society—a segment of society that includes 90 percent of our nation's children.

This book is not an indictment of public education. Nor is it a fan letter. It is an attempt to stimulate discussion and further a search for ways to promote positive moral values in our nation's public schools.

The first section explores the value problems facing public education by examining the need for a movement of moral reform in education, the various ways in which values are communicated, the history of values education, and the pervasive nature of values in education. The second section analyzes some of the opportunities and pitfalls of current school-reform efforts. The third section highlights several immediate, practical steps that parents and concerned Christians can take to make a difference in the schools.

The ten authors in this book bring a variety of views to the discussion. They may disagree with one another on the best course to restore values to public education. But they all agree the mission is vital.

Whether you and I like it or not, public schools will continue to play a major role in educating our nation's children. More than forty million children will pass through public classrooms this year. They will become the politicians and preachers, lawyers and reporters, executives and workers who create our society in years to come. If we are serious about doing something to deal with the fast-eroding moral base of our nation, we must realize that public schools offer parents, teachers, and concerned citizens a unique opportunity to transmit positive moral values, not only for the class of 2002, but for all future generations.

EXPLORING
THE PROBLEM

Chapter 1

NEW FUEL FOR SCHOOL REFORM

Ernest L. Boyer

School reform is not a new topic on the national agenda. The need for education—and debate about how best to accomplish the task—arrived with the first colonists. As early as 1642, the colony of Massachusetts passed a law requiring parents to see to the education of their children. Since then, waves of reform have come and gone, pushing schools in one direction and another.

As the size and influence of public education have grown, so have the expectations placed upon it. And so have its problems. Today, many say, schools are in a state of crisis. Their alarm has once again trained public attention on education, and reform measures are being debated and enacted across the country.

Ernest Boyer, president of the Carnegie Foundation for the Advance-

ment of Teaching, welcomes the renewed attention to our schools. But he sees a danger in the current push for improvement.

Are the problems our society faces today due to a lack of technical knowledge or a lack of moral wisdom to guide the use of such knowledge? Clearly, the greatest need lies in the formation of character in our young people. To meet that need, a moral-reform movement must begin to shape public education in the years ahead.

T he pursuit of excellence in public education has become a top priority for the nation. Since 1983, America has been engaged in the most serious and sustained push for school renewal in its history. In that year, the Department of Education's report *A Nation at Risk* sounded the alarm over the "rising tide of mediocrity" in our schools, and education reform became a hot topic from town halls to the halls of Congress.

The sense of urgency is well placed. Thirty years ago, the Soviets' launch of *Sputnik* touched off this country's last big push for school reform. We wanted scientists to compete in the space race and, given the Cold War climate of the day, children were bundled off into physics and chemistry classes, slide rules in hand, to assure that America would remain militarily secure.

This time, the reform movement has been driven almost exclusively by economic threats and by the growing recognition that without good schools the financial well-being of the nation is imperiled. Corporate leaders want better workers. Governors want industries in their states, and they know quality education is the key. We are trying to fix the schools to have a better work force and improve our competitive advantage in world markets.

No one denies that America's performance must improve. We talk enviously about Japanese schools and preach computer literacy for our students, all to help the nation take a quantum leap in the international high-tech race. Education and the economy are inextricably interlocked, and it is now argued that if the United States is to regain its competitive advantage, mind power is the key.

Civic priorities

But there is a danger in the current movement. While economic imperatives are being vigorously pursued, civic priorities are neglected. Study after study reveals that students in the nation's schools know little about the history of the United States and the institutions that sustain it. Further, there is a sharp decline in confidence in our civic institutions, and voter participation, especially among the younger generation, is falling off. Surely we need schools to educate America's work force; but we need an educated citizenry as well.

From the earliest days of this republic, schools have accepted the obligation of preparing young people to participate in the building of a nation. In 1816, Thomas Jefferson captured this inspired vision in a letter to a friend: "If a nation expects to be ignorant and free, in a state of civilization, it expects what never was and never will be."

The establishing of a network of common schools in the nineteenth century was, in large measure, an attempt to strengthen the democracy. The push for universal education was driven less by individual gain than by the desire to promote the social and civic advancement of the nation, based on the belief that we had, in this country, a rich heritage to be shared.

In the decade of the 1980s, E. D. Hirsch's *Cultural Literacy* and Allan Bloom's *The Closing of the American Mind* helped stir the conviction, once again, that a core curriculum is needed to sustain a common culture. There is a growing awareness that all citizens should have the capacity to read the morning newspaper thoughtfully, engage in public discourse, and understand key issues that will affect their lives from a perspective that is both national and global.

For those who care about government "by the people," the decline in public understanding cannot go unchallenged. In a world where human survival is at stake, ignorance is not an acceptable alternative. What we need today are groups of well-informed, caring individuals who band together in the spirit of community to learn from one another and to participate, as citizens, in the democratic process.

Several years ago, in the Carnegie report *High School*, we proposed that all students, regardless of their vocational objectives, complete a core program in literature, the arts, foreign language, history, civics, science, and mathematics in order to extend their knowledge and broaden their perspective. The nation's schools have a civic obligation to fulfill.

Moral wisdom
But there is still another crucial objective for our schools—*moral* education. Today, schools are instilling competence in their stu-

dents—competence in meeting deadlines, gathering information, responding well on tests, and mastering the details of a special field. The capacity to deal successfully with discrete problems is highly prized. And when students are asked about why they want an education, almost without exception they say their goal is to get a diploma and get a job.

But technical skill, of whatever kind, leaves open essential questions: Education for what purpose? Competence to what end? To have people who are well informed but not constrained by conscience is, perhaps, the most dangerous outcome of education. Indeed, it could be argued that ignorance is better than unguided intelligence, for the most dangerous people are those who have knowledge without a moral framework. It is not the lack of technological information that threatens our society; it is the lack of wisdom, and we run the risk today of having our discoveries outdistance our moral compass.

In medicine we know how to extend life beyond what might have been its natural limits. The question is, "At what point have we introduced more bad than good?" In business schools we turn out graduates who know how to make money on Wall Street, but we often fail to ask, "What is the right way to make money?"

Thus, the current reform movement should confront candidly the *moral* obligations of education. But what precisely does the term mean?

Moral education has to do with much more than a formal study of the history of ethical thought. It means helping students shape a way of behaving that will guide their lives, not just in a social sense, but in a personal sense as well. During their years of formal learning, students must understand that not all choices are equally valid. They must learn that there is a right and a wrong; that one choice will bring good, and another will bring bad.

Possessing moral judgment does not mean people are infallible, that they do not make mistakes. It does not suggest that there are pat answers for every complicated question. Moral education does mean that students should be concerned, not just about what will *work*, but about what is *right*. It means teaching them to ask: "Is it good?" Moral education also seeks to help students develop a responsible way of thinking, believing, *and* acting. It involves application, instead of mere information. It teaches living, not just by concepts, but by conscience.

All of this sounds fine—in principle—but how is it translated in the classroom? It is here that the meaning of moral education must be seriously confronted. Whose morality is the model? Where does education turn to secure the road map in helping students understand the good and the bad?

Respecting diversity

Through most of the nation's history, there was wide agreement among citizens on the "values" society should hold. What children learned in school reinforced the code of conduct that was taught at church and in the home. Indeed, the school was an extension of these institutions, and even the discipline of children was consistent. Almost everyone over the age of fifty can recall hearing, "If you get punished at school, you get spanked at home!" School values and home values were interlocked.

Some argue that there was, in fact, too much conformity in those days, that the "forced consensus" in the culture allowed for little deviation. It was a climate in which Roger Williams had to flee from the Massachusetts Bay Colony and found the colony of Rhode Island to find religious freedom, a time when Quakers were hanged because they deviated from what was religiously acceptable.

Today we have swung dramatically in the opposite direction. Our society is now characterized not by rigidity, but by such open-endedness that consensus seems, at times, almost impossible to reach.

This puts the nation's schools squarely in the middle. Administrators and teachers encounter problems because the national consensus regarding values has eroded, and tensions about teaching values in the schools reflect tensions in society at large. Schools are often confused—even abused—as they try to deal with competing interests and the great ambiguity about what constitutes the common good.

Amidst the diversity, however, there is still a great consensus in this nation about appropriate behavior. We can agree on the need to be honest, to respect the property of others, to refrain from physical attacks on one another, to obey the laws, to finish a task once begun—the list goes on and on. Schools teach these values every day and often reinforce them more effectively than society at large. Further, education itself is a value on which we all agree. It reflects the widely held conviction that knowledge is better than ignorance. The fact that we think children should learn to read and write reflects a value, just as do the content, arrangement, and procedures of every school day.

At one level, the nation's schools affirm every single day the widely shared values of our culture. And today one cannot find a school that does not teach students, directly or indirectly, that it is better to be honest than dishonest; that it is better to be courteous than discourteous; that it is better to work hard than not work at all; that it is better to respect someone's property than to destroy it. Schools teach our children a way of life that is shared by almost all Americans.

But again, there are areas of ambiguity in society. Schools are often criticized for not probing the hotly contested issues, and they are also criticized if they do!

Consider an issue as seemingly innocent as the American family. Such a study could well include a discussion of mothers working outside the home. In discussing working mothers, is the teacher encouraging young women to work instead of caring for their children? On the other hand, if homemaking is proposed, the teacher may be criticized for advocating second-class status for women by pushing them into stereotypical roles. Society is far from consensus on the subject; thus, tensions emerge. Yet to ignore the issue—or any issue of similar controversy—is to offer students an incomplete education, an incapacity to think carefully about life's most important concerns.

The efforts of schools to respect a wide range of opinion in matters of faith and practice should be celebrated, not carelessly condemned. Indeed, to support diversity, to resist oppression and mass conformity, is exactly what drove many immigrant citizens to this country. Believers of all faiths should understand and appreciate this freedom. We should be very hesitant to impose, through uniform school practice, any behavior that cuts the conscience of another. Tomorrow, it could be our turn.

All of us can remember times when a conviction we hold dear

conflicted with the majority view. When I was a boy, my parents, as a matter of conscience, did not approve of vaccinations. They believed that faith in God was all the power needed to keep me healthy. Because the school required proof that I had been vaccinated from contagious disease, I had to get a doctor's certificate granting me an exception. I was the only boy in school—a very definite minority—who needed such accommodation. But it was granted (I have since, by the way, been vaccinated).

Though my conflict was a minor one, it nevertheless was a collision between my parents' conscience and established policy. In my own small way I saw, firsthand, the conflict faced by those who hold views at odds with the established action. And I felt the sting of other students and teachers who did not understand. Let us not judge too harshly a school where differences are defended.

I do not suggest a prohibition against the teaching of controversial issues. Schools face a dilemma, however, when they confront issues about which convictions run the deepest, yet vary the widest. And yet, increasingly, we ask schools to enter society's hottest controversies—debates in which there is no neutral ground to be found. How are schools to handle moral dilemmas when there is no agreement in the community and among parents on what the response should be?

Once a conviction is widely shared and generally resolved, the schools will teach it. But until such time, schools inevitably will fail to satisfy the expectations of some part of the public they serve. And most teachers understandably are inclined to conclude that some topics are simply too hot to handle.

Filling the moral vacuum
Still, I am convinced that schools *do* have a role to play in moral education, one that goes beyond silence or the extension of the status quo. Schools are, by their very nature, creative and renewing institutions. There is undeniably a moral vacuum in society today, and educators have an urgent obligation to help fill it.

I am encouraged to see a small but growing awareness of the need for moral education, and a willingness to explore issues, even in the areas that are most contested. From classroom teachers across the country to the president of Harvard University, people are asking, "What can schools do to help students achieve higher ethical standards?" I have no master plan to renew the moral climate in public education. That is a discussion to which the remaining chapters of this book contribute. I do, however, offer three suggestions that I feel must guide any consideration of moral education in our schools.

First, such effort should acknowledge and respect the diversity present in our society. Finding a way to deal with our differences, while still speaking of values that serve the common good, is the greatest challenge we confront. How can we find creative ways to instill moral sensibilities in our young people while still respecting differing points of view? An amoral silence that ignores the common good for the sake of diversity has failed. So, too, have the shrill voices that presume to speak for all, but speak selfishly without thoughtfulness and kindness. Let us cherish our diversity, but let us seek with no less vigor a way of life that uplifts us all.

Second, we must nurture a rebirth of confidence in public schools. If we are to make any progress toward open and sensitive classroom discussion about moral choices—in such controversial areas as sex, drugs, and religious beliefs—teachers must be trusted. A school is not a building or an institution; it is people. I urge those who care deeply about education to do one thing: meet with those who run the schools and talk with them directly.

Throughout the years, I have met with thousands of teachers in hundreds of schools and have found, overwhelmingly, that the educators care deeply about the values of our children. Teachers are, in fact, mothers and fathers, brothers and sisters, aunts and uncles— ordinary people who have a deep concern about children and the nation. I know of no teacher who thinks that values are unimportant. There is no conspiracy at work in public schools to deny our children an ethical and moral foundation.

Teachers want children to do what is right, and they are most concerned about the moral ambiguity of the culture that washes over into the climate of the schools. In a recent Carnegie Foundation survey of teachers, we found them deeply frustrated by the lack of involvement of parents in schools. Parental concerns will always be welcomed when they come from those who approach schools with an appreciation for the limits of public education, in a spirit of cooperation, with affirmation and encouragement when deserved.

A place for involvement

Finally, we must view moral education as a partnership, not an obligation for the schools to carry alone. I hear complaints that schools are undermining values. But what I find surprising is the way these same critics seem to express little faith in what families can accomplish.

All the evidence suggests that, in the end, parents matter most, and it is unfair to families—as well as schools—to expect classrooms to do the whole job. I am not trying to take schools off the hook. They have an important role to play in the moral development of children. But we cannot expect schools to do what families have not been able to accomplish.

The church also can play a valuable, redemptive role merely by taking the initiative to listen, rather than denounce. Churches can work side by side with schools to educate their young people through released-time and after-school programs. There is a long history of such cooperation in this country, which unfortunately seems lost in much of the current discussion about how to strengthen moral education.

Congregations and small groups should invite teachers to speak at churches and synagogues about their feelings and experiences. Such simple measures will go a long way in restoring confidence and a sense of partnership with schools.

Today we stand at a strategic time in the history of public education. Interest in schools has run high during the past several years. But public attention cannot be indefinitely sustained. And if we do not demonstrate clearly within the next ten years our ability to make public education work, there will be, I fear, a tremendous backlash of disillusionment. Our schools will be neglected, parents will turn away in discouragement, and the very future of the nation will be threatened.

This window of opportunity hinges to a great extent on the ability of the schools to pursue not just the economic and civic ends of education, but to affirm moral education, too. I sense a growing conviction that this country confronts increasing confusion over goals, and if schools are not part of the solution, they will be part of the problem. People are not willing to support education that does not inspire students to confront ethical and moral judgments and relate what they learn in school to how they live.

When all is said and done, the nation's schools should encourage each student to develop the capacity to judge wisely in matters of life and conduct. Time must be taken in classrooms to explore ambiguities and reflect on the imponderables of life. The goal is not to indoctrinate students, but to provide a climate in which ethical and moral choices can be thoughtfully examined, and convictions formed. These are the characteristics by which, ultimately, the quality of public education must be measured.

Chapter 2

GETTING THE MORAL MESSAGE ACROSS

Ted Ward

"What we have here is a failure to communicate," goes the line from a popular movie, a saying that might well be applied to efforts to instill moral values in children. Developing a clear, effective set of values is difficult enough for adults. *But passing those values on to the next generation? The task frustrates even the most dedicated parents.*

Schools face the same difficult job, compounded by confusion over constitutional rights and church-state relations. Before any discussion of values education can go too far, the question must be addressed: How are values communicated?

In this chapter, Ted Ward, who during thirty years of teaching at Michigan State University directed the Values Development Education

Center, describes four ways in which moral values can be communicated. Christians, says Ward, now professor of missions and Christian education at Trinity Evangelical Divinity School, tend to focus on only one means of communication. The result is not only an inaccurate assessment of the moral education that can and does take place in public schools, but also an incomplete understanding of the purpose of moral education.

T he broad term *values* can refer to any preference or choice: liking chocolate ice cream rather than vanilla, or preferring a Ford over a Chevrolet. All such expressions of likes and dislikes are value statements. What makes a value a *moral* value? Moral values deal specifically with choices that involve human welfare. A more elaborate definition than that could be offered, but at their heart, moral values deal with the welfare of human beings—of one person, or a whole society. For example, an incident of assault involves moral values, because the welfare of another is affected. It is easy to see how pervasive moral values are, because so many acts of daily living affect the well-being of others.

Can schools influence the values of their students? The question is hardly worth asking; its answer is obvious. It is *impossible* to put a child in sustained contact with an adult without the adult exerting some kind of moral influence on the child. All teachers—and teachers are the heart of our educational system—influence values, for better or worse.

Most teachers are consciously aware that they influence the moral values of their students. And certainly most good teachers realize the power of their influence. So the question to start with is not *can* schools affect children morally, but in what ways *do* schools—and the whole process of education—affect children?

Thou shalt not . . .
There are four ways in which moral values are communicated. The first and perhaps most obvious way is by stating them as propositions—the explicit naming and declaring of value statements. For example, when a teacher says, "It is wrong to copy from someone else's test paper," she is teaching a moral value.

This is the method of communicating values most familiar to many Christians; it is found throughout Scripture in the form of commands. Because of their well-placed emphasis on the biblical texts, Christians value a heavy use of Scripture in any teaching of moral values. An unfortunate result of this emphasis is that when they evaluate moral education in schools, they often search exclusively for explicit statements of moral values. And if they fail to find them they conclude that values education is not taking place.

Such preoccupation with this single means of communication is unfortunate for two reasons: First, it ignores the other means through which values can be communicated. Second, teaching values as propositions has many limitations.

Take, for example, the memorization of the Ten Commandments. I would never argue that it is useless to memorize the Ten Commandments. But even the Decalogue is not an adequately spelled-out list for every situation. Consider the eighth commandment, "Thou shalt not steal." What does stealing include? We apply it to a huge manifest of other things that we do not even call stealing. We talk about copying, or cheating on tests, or plagiarism. Those transgressions are embraced by the general command against stealing.

However, that is not the way children learn it. They learn that it is not right to look at the answers on someone else's test paper. To them, that is the law against cheating on tests. They learn that it is not right to copy homework from a classmate. That is the law against copying. Even having learned the Mosaic statements by heart, one still faces the question of how "Thou shalt not steal" applies to cheating on a test.

The limitations of teaching values only as propositional statements often become evident in encounters with people of different cultures. Muslims, for example, have very strict laws against stealing. But Muslims also learn from an early age that one of the highest compliments one can give to another—even to Allah—is to quote him. In fact, quoting others is such a compliment that one need not credit the source; one merely repeats the words or ideas.

"That is plagiarism!" Americans say. "It is dishonest." So when an American teacher grades an Arab student's paper and finds unattributed quotations, she marks it down. But the thought that such a practice might be against the rules of a school may never have occurred to a Muslim. Islam prohibits stealing, but plagiarism is not seen as a matter of "taking without permission." There is not even a concept of "plagiarism," let alone the idea that it is somehow wrong.

Another example comes from the commandment "Thou shalt not bear false witness." In other words, "Tell the truth." Children are constantly put in a dilemma with reference to telling the truth. Telling the truth, in the language of the American court system, talks about "the whole truth and nothing but the truth." But a child grows up with a great deal of ambiguity about when to tell the truth because, among other things, he or she is also told not to tattle. Simply having the value statement "Tell the truth" does not help the child understand why, when he tells the teacher that Charlie is chewing gum, he may be scolded for tattling. The issue of truthfulness gets confused in the socializing task of a parent or teacher who is trying to dissuade the child from using truth hurtfully toward others. Such a moral dilemma is not solved simply by naming the rules.

So the *naming of a value*, apart from any connection with its manifestations in life, is a very limited exercise. The matter of moral values goes far beyond the issue of knowing what a value statement looks like, or even knowing which values are right, or godly, or Christian.

Is there a place for naming values? There is, indeed. But more important is the *behavior* of that value. Naming it is the icing on the cake.

Teacher, I love you
The second way moral values are communicated is by relationship. There comes a moment early in the career of almost every teacher— often as early as a student-teaching experience—when he or she is struck by the relationship of teacher and student. That moment often goes something like this: Jill has been a student teacher in a second-grade classroom for two weeks. Just before recess a little girl comes up, takes her by the hand, leans up against her, and says, "Miss Johnson, I love you," and skips out to recess.

There is an electricity in that moment when the teacher realizes that that child is involved with her. That little girl is paying attention to what the teacher does and says; there is an emotional attachment to her. Jill Johnson had not necessarily been working for that, but it was there.

Older children have more elaborate ways of showing this attachment. But they show it, particularly in terms of wanting the approval of the teacher. Teachers in all kinds of schools discover early on that many children pay attention to whether or not they are pleasing the teacher. Even in "tough" schools, even with "hard" kids, even with kids who might seem hopeless, the teacher who knows how to read those little signals recognizes the tremendous potential for moral influence he or she has on a student.

The teaching relationship with students is a powerful influence. It can be used for godly purposes: for righteousness, justice, truth. Or it can be used for the antithesis of godliness. Teachers need the persistent encouragement of God's people to use their influence well.

Christians can easily recognize the important potential for communicating values through positive relationships. One of the most powerful means to bring people to Christ is by showing personal interest in them. As a matter of fact, the first time a whole community was brought to Christ, the evangelizing message was, to paraphrase, "Come, see a man who has told me everything about myself"; in other words, "a man who has shown a deep interest in me" (John 4:39).

In a private school, a public school, or a Christian school, wherever there is a godly person in the teaching role, there is a potential for a godly influence on a life through *relationship*. And any environment that allows a person to live in a consistent, upright manner offers the opportunity for powerful, positive moral influence.

Recent court decisions have impinged upon various expressions of faith, such as prayers at the start of the school day or before athletic events. In one recent decision, a teacher was told he could not have an open Bible on his desk. Those decisions are lamentable, and in many cases unfair and misguided. But such emblems of Christian behavior are, frankly, beside the point in discussing the communication of moral values. We must be careful not to transfer the focus of Christianity from its heart—a personal relationship with Jesus Christ—to the emblems and the labels of that relationship.

Unless in some tragic, future moment it becomes impossible for a Christian to be faithful to Christ in the public school, the public school will continue to be an appropriate and accessible arena for the communication of Christian values. As long as Christians are free to relate positively to people and demonstrate love and concern, we are free to be as Christ's sheep in Matthew 25, who by showing compassion to one of "the least of these," did so to Christ himself, and so entered into his kingdom.

Something to talk about

The third way moral values are communicated is through counseling. Children seek out an adult with whom they are comfortable, but sharing their problems with an adult can be very difficult. School provides for children the opportunity for just such counseling, but the effectiveness depends on the openness of the teacher.

Many Christian teachers are ready and willing to help children with their moral dilemmas. Seldom, however, is it called "counseling." More often it is called "Mr. Hughes, I've got something I want to talk with you about." And children will spend all the time a teacher is willing to give them in this regard.

Good teachers—and Christian teachers, especially—are willing to give the time needed. Most parents would be surprised to learn how true that is. Teachers talk with one another about their concerns for kids more often than most of us realize.

From the perspective of Christians truly concerned about moral values in education, one of the great strengths of the public-school environment is the opportune location, situation, and context it provides Christian teachers to be available to children, available in many ways to many people who would otherwise never be reachable.

Putting the pieces together

The fourth way moral values are communicated in education is through the whole effect of the school's curriculum, which in American public education includes far more than just books.

Often, critics of public education focus on the textbooks used in schools. They decry, for example, the absence of values or religion in the texts. The omission of such vital parts of our historic and contemporary experience is indeed troubling. But what the critics tend to overlook is the teacher. In public education, a broad definition of curriculum takes into account more than just printed materials; curriculum includes texts and teachers and other students (see chapter 9, "Beyond the Lesson Plan: Curriculum and Values"). A good teacher puts the pieces together, often providing the elements missing from a book.

As they play their part in the curriculum, teachers can communicate and influence values in three ways.

Influence through issue-oriented discussions. One of the positive features of public education in the United States is that the schools are free to deal with issues, and are not restricted simply to passing on books full of material from one generation to the next. That freedom means that virtually every teacher from the first grade onward—if that teacher has any creative wits at all—spends part of the day in issue-oriented discussions with students.

This happens across the board, in elementary schools and high schools alike. For example, when a conflict between first graders arises, the typical teacher will most likely approach the situation with questions: "Johnny, why did you do that? Do you think that was the right thing to do?"

At first glance, a line of questions may seem of little worth in communicating moral values. But trained teachers can be much more effective in the use of questions than a Sunday school teacher who fears discussion. Frankly, one persistent problem in church education is that teachers—volunteer teachers—are so uneasy with discussions that they tend to monopolize class time with monologues. Most public-school teachers are not at all threatened by discussion and will open the floor to children. Yes, kids will say some strange things. But they will also say some wise things.

The emphasis here on what kids *say* is quite intentional. People do not learn values by hearing about them. They learn by *doing*; and further, they learn to evaluate their own values by talking about them. Presuming that attitudes can be altered by listening to lectures is a common mistake of parents and beginning teachers. "Men loved darkness rather than light, because their deeds were evil" (John 3:19) says it very well. Behavior and experience with evil results in loving darkness. One of the tasks of moral education must be to help people discover the way their behavior gives birth to values and feelings.

One of the things a Christian teacher can do is intentionally give time and space for the Christian kids to say *their* piece. Not unfairly, or preferentially, but allowing them to voice clearly their basis of wisdom—biblical wisdom.

Influence through choices of emphasis. Most adults can remember from their own school days how toward the end of the term some teachers would go into a panic because they had not covered all the material in one of the textbooks. In most nations of the world that cannot happen. In France, for example, each teacher is required to stay on the national schedule—exactly which pages are to be covered on each and every school day is spelled out for every teacher. Teachers in America, however, have a great deal of latitude in almost every subject, with the exception of certain skills, such as typing. In general, they are free to choose what they will emphasize during their teaching time—what they will spend more time on, or less time on; what will be discussed, what will be ignored, what will be tested.

That *emphasis* in the handling of curriculum—especially in the humanities, history, and literature—plays a big role in whether a student is able to see the moral message of an assignment. Teachers on the whole are very inventive people. The best teachers are known for teaching in a creative way, putting those emphases together in ways that capture children's imaginations. Only the timid beginner or lazy old-timer simply stays with the book. The creative teacher takes advantage of those freedoms to create emphases that reflect his or her values.

Influence through the "here's how I see it" explanation. Teachers should, and to a large degree do, avoid dictating their own value statements to students. But many opportunities arise in well-chosen moments to say with sensitivity and respect, "I guess that might be the way some people see it, but here's how I see it."

The wise teacher does not lead that sentence with, "The Bible says," but over time, youngsters working with such a teacher become conscious that these ideas come from somewhere specific. And in time, after a teacher has built a moral base of wisdom by comments made to the class, he or she has a legitimate occasion to acknowledge the source of that wisdom.

That is very different from starting with a Scripture verse. For example, a teacher could say "In Romans 3:23 it says 'all have sinned and fall short of the glory of God.' " That is a statement of proposition. Or that teacher could use another approach, saying, "Here's how I see it: There is evil in this world, there always has been, there always will be, because people tend to do things their own way. The evil that is in this world results in bad things for people. People keep looking inside themselves to find better ways to do things, and they cannot find them."

Quite typically, when you lead kids that far they will say "Okay, where would you turn?" and that is the time for a wisely chosen "here's how I see it. . . ." Few public-relations problems are generated by that kind of representation of godliness.

The crises that grab headlines generally come when somebody is trying to start a conflict. But some teachers believe that it is more important to *teach* than to fight. They avoid arguments that are sure to become "bait" for conflict. Instead, they keep the emphasis on the students and their concerns.

This approach served me well for thirty years at Michigan State University. Admittedly, a public university is different from an elementary school or high school. But no administrator challenged me, no department chairman warned me, no one attacked me for the overt Christianity expressed through my teaching. I was not silent about it, but I was not sparring for a fight. I was content to let the structure of a carefully built moral position emerge and then give credit where it was due, rather than the other way around.

The goal of moral education
In evaluating the various means of communicating values, what is perhaps most important to consider is the objective of values education. As Christians, our concern should reach far beyond the mere pronouncement of value statements. The goal of moral education must include not only producing in our children the capability of judging right from wrong, but creating in them the desire and ability to live according to those judgments.

The issue, therefore, is not just whether a teacher is free to name values and require their memorization. Again, doing so is by no means wrong, nor useless. But it is not as vital, for example, to have students memorize the Ten Commandments as it is to help them develop the moral behavior and moral consciousness that the Ten Commandments represent. The main task of values education is the walk of life based on godly values. Certainly no Christian would be satisfied with a moral education in which people learned to name godly values but developed no concern for appropriate behavior.

Can schools teach godliness, even when they do not call it godliness? When students and teachers create an orderly society in the school in which people can live and operate in mutual respect while they pursue truth, they are in fact conveying Christian values. For where does the godliness of a value lie—in the name of that value, or in the value itself?

Stealing dishonors God. And even when the commandment is not stated in so many words, its truth remains. So when a teacher is teaching children not to steal, the teacher is nonetheless communicating that godly value. Whether it is a godly value or not does not depend on who is communicating; neither does it depend on the label attached to it. The value is like a Christmas present; its worth resides not in the tag, but in the present itself.

To continue with that analogy, however, there is a purpose for tags. They identify the giver of a present. And a time eventually comes when knowing the source of the values is important. Sooner or later, as every child becomes an individual, he or she will begin to ask, How do I know this is an important value? How do I know this is a true value, or is it simply a value that somebody in my past believed and passed along to me?

If there is a failing of public education in reference to moral values, it is this: that the present confusion about constitutional rights does not encourage teachers to ground the values they teach in explicit reference to their sources.

There remain, however, many ways to communicate moral values. God is concerned about more than how well we reason through moral questions or recite lists of values. God is concerned about our moral actions. Effective moral education will shape actions as well as attitudes. And to be effective, it must make use of every means of communication available.

Chapter 3

WHERE HAVE THE VALUES GONE?

R. Lewis Hodge

In the mid-1940s, a California police and education officials survey asked public school teachers what their top discipline problems were. The list of answers included talking, chewing gum, running, making noise in the halls, and getting out of turn in line. In the mid-1980s, the same question brought these responses: rape, robbery, assault, burglary, suicide, drug and alcohol abuse, and arson.

How could the moral climate of our public schools change so drastically in such a short time? Lewis Hodge, associate professor of education at the University of Tennessee–Knoxville, examines the past forty years to identify the significant developments that have shaped public education and its approach to the teaching of values. Societal attitudes and expectations, court decisions, educational philosophies, theories of moral development—all have contributed to the schools' current quandary over moral education.

The heart of the problem, Hodge explains, is not a disappearance of values. On the contrary, schools face a proliferation of values in an increasingly diverse culture. At the same time, Christians through several generations have failed to influence society through constructive participation in its institutions, such as public education. We can best begin seeking solutions for the problems of the present by studying their past.

Many Americans believe that public schools no longer teach values as they should. Christians in particular have complained that students are permitted and even encouraged to live by values that are inconsistent with those of basic Christian belief, resulting in an erosion of the moral quality of life in America. Many non-Christians also decry the loss of "traditional values."

Where have the values gone? A review of the past forty years, focusing on only a few significant developments, reveals above all that the "value problem" of public education today has not been created by the disappearance of values; rather, it is the result of the growth of myriad disparate values.

America's once clearly Judeo-Christian context has been reshaped in this century by a pervasive emphasis upon individual freedoms, by the addition and growth of many diverse subcultures,[1] and by the pluralism of Christianity itself.[2] Together, these forces have created a culture distinctively more complex than that of two centuries, or even a few decades ago. Both secular and Christian pluralism have effectively diluted our Judeo-Christian values. The net effect, at least from the point of view of many Christians, has been to create the appearance of a culture and its public schools that are value free, when, in fact, both are value saturated.

Christianity in withdrawal

The expanding complexity and trend toward secularity of twentieth-century American culture were already in motion by the end of the 1800s. And Christians themselves, it should be noted, contributed as much as any group to the decline of religious influence and the rise of secularism. Churches that adhered to Christian orthodoxy ("fundamentalists," as they came to be called) determined to resist the perceived social trends toward pragmatism and materialism and withdrew from the culture at large. As a result, a significant portion of Christendom went into withdrawal—or "separation," as they preferred to call it—from mainstream American culture.[3]

Public schools followed the American culture through the first half of the twentieth century, and the Christian influence that had been diminishing since the Civil War was further subdued. The secular tide ebbed and flowed through World War I, the Roaring Twenties, the Great Depression, and a second world war.

Religious (Judeo-Christian) values continued, but they did so through their conversion, for all practical purposes, into "traditional values." For example, distinctively Christian concepts such as *sin*, *righteousness*, *grace*, and *love*, became *wrong*, *right*, *compassion*, and *caring*, respectively. Many other Christian virtues became traditional values: honesty, respect, courage, good humor, and any number of a long list of traits that could be drawn from various codes of ethics, such as the Boy Scout code or the Cardinal Principles of Secondary Education.

Another example of this transformation is found in how the concept of marriage changed from the Judeo-Christian idea of "holy matrimony" to a more traditional view of it as a formal, long-term commitment. (The next step was the concept of marriage as a legal relationship: often a written contract with termination rights and property division.)

Whatever reservations Christians may have had by mid-century, these traditional values seemed to create a golden age for contemporary Christianity—at least to many Christians today who view that era with nostalgia. The predominant values of society, by whatever name, remained recognizable and acceptable to Christians. At least in appearance and practice, traditional values were not significantly different from their religious counterparts. But their foundation was increasingly pragmatic and functional, rather than philosophical or religious; the following decade would reveal how weak the infrastructure of traditional values had become.

Schooling of the 1950s seemed "a golden age" as well. The relative unity in the postwar period (Americans had pulled together as never before to defeat the evils represented by the Axis powers) was embodied in the public schools. They were the common vehicle for transmitting American values, providing rich and poor with opportunities for acquiring knowledge and skills, and literally bringing together the majority of the child population.[4]

In short, public schools in the fifties were, as they had long been, a common denominator among Americans. They became institutions of compromise, in which the increasingly diverse population worked out its differences. Out of that ongoing compromise emerged a common set of values, a "civil religion" as some have called it,[5] that affirmed traditional values and promoted other ideals. Students of the day were taught to work hard, because hard work guaranteed success. They were expected to do their own work with very little outside assistance. The standards were high; students met them, or got red-penciled *F*s for failure.

Such a civil religion looked tolerantly upon Christianity. Furthermore, many teachers, community leaders, and citizens involved with their local schools were themselves Christians or were sympathetic to Christianity, or at least to traditional values. So Christians still had a discernible influence upon the public schools. Christians who could comfortably dwell in the American culture could for the most part endorse the public schools.

Scientific thinking

In the late 1950s, a single, dramatic event prompted changes— changes that altered the country's whole way of thinking, as well as its school curriculum. The Soviet Union's launch of *Sputnik* challenged all that America stood for, including its values (and particularly, its national pride and assumed responsibility to oppose anti-Christian communism, which secular and Christian Americans united to combat). In response, a new curriculum was developed, one designed to restore the nation to its former status of worldwide superiority. And how was education to accomplish that restoration? By producing scientists.

The space race, however, did much more to the country than turn out fledgling rocket scientists. With an emphasis on math, physics, and chemistry, came curricula in other fields that encouraged students to become more "scientific" in their thinking. Scientific inquiry became the pattern of virtually all education: Question existing knowledge, formulate new theories, search for and collect information, analyze data, accept or reject the theories, repeat the cycle. Science became the new guide to truth: Truth comes by discovery; discovery never ends. And with the rise of science, the long-standing tension between science and religion (and values based on revelation) was reinforced.[6]

The inquiry approach was extended, for example, to social studies. Instead of simply learning what tradition passed down, students were encouraged to follow the pattern of scientific inquiry. While this approach encouraged less ethnocentric thinking (which might please Christians who value the kingdom of God over any kingdom of man), it also encouraged the questioning of America's traditional values—not to mention Christian values.

A prime example of the inquiry approach to social studies was a high-quality curriculum called "Man, a Course of Study."[7] The struggle over its acceptance was not headline news, but the behind-the-scenes debate was so intense between liberal and conservative factions that the curriculum was eventually dropped; it was too volatile for both the curriculum publishers and further government funding.

Thus, *Sputnik* and the new curricula it prompted set the stage for the radical changes in "values education" that were to come in the 1960s and 1970s.

The never-ending search
"Will We Ever Get Over the '60s?" asked the cover of *Newsweek* magazine over 20 years after that tumultuous decade. Vietnam. The sexual revolution. Civil rights. Assassinations. Some of the changes wrought in that era were positive; some were negative. But somewhere along the way, in the midst of all the turmoil, a new primary value emerged as the sum of the cultural changes of the sixties and the years before. Without doubt, a new cultural presupposition became thoroughly evident during that decade: There is not, and cannot be, one true theory, culture, or religion. Furthermore, said the thinking of that day, each and every theory, culture, or religion has a right to exist if it can function effectively (basically an empirical argument). These presuppositions besieged existing standards and traditions, changing viewpoints heard from coffee shops to the Supreme Court.[8]

Combined with the post-*Sputnik* devotion to the "scientific approach," these new presuppositions produced a related and equally prevalent truism: Knowledge overwhelms wisdom. Knowledge, after all, can be "proven" through an accumulation of facts. Wisdom cannot be proven, and furthermore, can be refuted on the grounds of "cultural bias." Traditional values were easily cast aside. Two common questions accompanied the skepticism of the decade. The first, *Whom can we trust?* was answered: No one. And the second, *What values can we trust?* was answered similarly: None. So a generation searched for answers in an increasingly materialistic society, and found only quantifiable facts and shifting biases.

Arising from the milieu was an educational innovation that has come to be seen as the epitome of the relativistic thinking of the day: values clarification (VC).[9] With the publication of the book *Value and Teaching* in 1966, Louis Raths, Merrill Harmin, and Sidney Simon provided a new methodology to help children "arrive at their own values."[10]

Based on the premise that values are personal, this "value neutral" approach was widely adopted to foster discussion and introspection among children. Values clarification was based upon several assumptions: Traditional indoctrination is inadequate in today's culture; there are no absolute values to build upon; responsible values can be developed in the kinds of discussions VC promotes; human reason will best lead to individual value development anyway; and thus the child becomes better equipped to adapt to changing cultural norms.

Given its aims of clarifying values, teachers of values clarification are not supposed to reject even "bad values." If, for example, a group of fifth-graders determines through the VC process that lying to their parents is acceptable "for the right reasons," then a teacher should respect that decision.

In spite of Christians' long-running criticism of VC, there may be some common ground between religious aims and VC processes. In fairness to the approach, it should be noted as well that teachers, in their assigned role as mere facilitators of discussion, were *not* to squelch traditional values, just as they were not to judge any value. Individual teachers who believe in universal or absolute truths have been able to adapt and utilize VC methods and exercises to suit their purposes.

In addition, VC advocates assume that the American culture will continue to change and that survival and success are dependent not upon well-ingrained values but upon adaptable ones. Religious persons may agree there is a need to change their specific responses to the shifting culture, although their responses will always be based upon a given set of truths and principles. Discussion can strengthen the application of values to daily living.

The basic assumptions of values clarification, however, remain at odds with Christian or traditional values by declaring that no value or truth is universal or absolute (or self-evident, as the Declaration of Independence states).[11] And so, just as the culture of the sixties shunned transcendent values, education opened itself to the ever-shifting whims of personal preferences.

Thinking their way to values

Out of the confusion of the 1960s came the desire in the seventies for stability. But the mindset of the previous two decades led to a new base for cultural norms and values: knowledge. Judeo-Christian values had been subordinated as religious (or philosophically biased) and therefore unscientific. Traditional values were for yesterday's generation. So in the 1970s, the study of values took on a cognitive (from the Latin *cognitio*, meaning "knowledge") emphasis that portrayed morality as moral reasoning.

Concern over the confusion in the public schools of the sixties brought public outcries for a return to the basics of learning. The pursuit of knowledge continued, but students did not seem to be learning as much and as well as they could. Behavioral and cognitive social-science researchers provided help.

For example, psychologist J. P. Guilford's comprehensive model of learning (which he termed "the structure of intellect") posited 120 "cells," or discreet, intellectual functions, each of which, he said, could be systematically studied.[12] Guilford and many others approached learning as an orderly process that could be enhanced through scientific methods.

One of the most influential cognitive psychologists was Jean Piaget, a Swiss biologist turned psychologist, who determined that children go through stages of learning.[13] Piaget described the mental progression of children through general stages of development from concrete to more abstract thinking. When applied to education, understanding the stages and processes of cognitive development helps teachers know how to help students learn.

Building on the work of Piaget during the sixties and into the seventies, Harvard psychologist Lawrence Kohlberg became one of the foremost authorities on moral development and perhaps the biggest single influence on values education in the 1970s. Every person, Kohlberg believed, adult and child alike, is a "moral philosopher." In complex and comprehensive yet explainable ways, he wrote, an individual may advance across five stages from selfishness ("punishment and obedience") through socially conscious levels of moral development toward universal ethical principles ("conscience and respect for the rights, life, and dignity of all persons"; as evidenced, for example, in the lives of Jesus and Socrates). Studies conducted in many countries and cultures confirmed Kohlberg's and his disciples' beliefs that they were onto "universal truth" about how humans develop morally.

Christians have responded both positively and negatively to Kohlberg's theory.[14] Generally, Kohlberg's work seems adaptable, but not adoptable, for there are several points of disagreement with orthodox Christian teaching. For example, Jesus' teachings have no authority in Kohlberg's system. And there is no place for the concept of sin;[15] people like Hitler are not explained as evil but as people who did not develop correctly.

Christians also may ask who or what is the final authority in Kohlberg's influential scheme? The answer, in so many words, is human reasoning. By it the individual is vested with even greater control—the right and the power—to set his or her own values (an echo of the sixties). Again, the freedom for diversity increased, and public schools—the institution of compromise and accommodation—could only reflect the myriad views.

Values education at work

By the time the 1980s arrived, public schools faced a population quite different from that of the fifties. Schools continued to operate with a set of "institutional values" necessary to regulate classroom attendance and teacher-student relationships. Some schools, located in neighborhoods that remained relatively cohesive and somewhat traditional, promoted common understandings of expectations and behavior. In other schools that served more diverse populations, teachers were reticent to say or do anything that might offend a student and result in confrontation with students or parents. Public schools favored a posture of avoiding moral concerns, or of dealing with them in such a relativistic way as to render them meaningless.

Values continue to be taught and demonstrated in the public school, sometimes akin to the fifties, but often in careful, selective ways. Basic values like responsibility, honesty, and respect have not disappeared, but they are often practiced differently than in years past. For example, cheating continues to be wrong. However, the suspension likely in the fifties has been moderated in the eighties. Why? Because in the eighties, there are students—and parents—who perceive cheating not as a moral wrong, but as a kind of game in which the object is to avoid getting caught. In such a moral climate, the difficulties of proving the offense and then taking action to discourage it are obvious.

The typical classroom setting of today is often a "moral stalemate." What goes on is basically cognitive; affective learning is too risky—personally and professionally. One comprehensive study of American public schools observed the "flat, neutral emotional ambience of most of the classes" it studied,[16] the abiding emphasis on accumulating facts and practicing basic skills. "It is difficult to be sanguine about the moral and ethical learnings accompanying many of the experiences of schooling," writes John Goodlad, author of *A Place Called School.* "My perception is that the emphasis on individual performance and achievement would be more conducive to cheating than to the development of moral integrity.... Particularly lacking in our data is anything to suggest the deliberate involvement of students in making moral judgments and in understanding the difference between these and decisions based on scientific facts."[17]

Responses to Goodlad's summation have been undertaken by various schools during the eighties—in spite of their otherwise jumbled approach to values. Of particular interest for this discussion are the responses of Christians. Some say values training has no place in the schools; their emphasis should be upon the cognitive aspects of schooling, as Goodlad (and most other educators) believe it is. Other Christians argue that such a cognitive emphasis is indeed the crux of the problem; it is the cause of education's failure to develop character.

Particular programs have been offered toward the latter end: to develop character. For example, the Clovis (Calif.) Unified School District has devised its own model student, the Clovis Sparthenian, who is honest, responsible, respectful, dedicated, perseverant, self-respecting, and concerned for others. The program's broad-based approach uses teachers, selected class content, school citizenship programs, and other existing constructs to impart these characteristics.

Baltimore city schools are participating with Johns Hopkins University and Coppin State College in a program to train literature teachers to teach moral values and moral reasoning dialectically through a study of Plato's *Republic*, Dante's *The Divine Comedy*, and Alexis de Tocqueville's *Democracy in America*.

In Oxford, Ohio, the school board has approved "Moral Guidelines," a list of 21 statements affirming such attributes as self-discipline, honesty, and respect.

While these examples show that values in education have hardly disappeared, they also illustrate that there is no nationwide values curriculum, nor any national trend in values in education akin to the recent movement emphasizing "basic skills." The subject does appear, however, to be gaining interest. Several academic books and a number of journal publications dealing with moral education and character development have appeared in the late 1980s. Even the return of the word *character* to the professional literature is significant, for many psychologists and psychiatrists do not officially recognize the concept as viable.

Two conclusions

In this century, America has gradually moved from familiar Christian values to more traditional values to a plurality of values. A scientific, empirical shift in the curriculum followed by an emphasis upon the pursuit of technical knowledge have been instrumental in the perceived crisis in "values in education." Our culture, and our schools with it, have arrived at a scientific age. But as Goodlad's summation indicates, the scientific process is not a satisfactory means for determining values. The changes in values during this century have been a mixture of "good" and "bad" (depending on one's point of view). Many Christians perceive a loss of influence upon the public schools—even a rejection. But it would be more accurate to say that Christian influence has been diluted. What does the future hold? Sociologist Robert Bellah[18] has addressed the tension of the individual versus society, and educational historian Freeman Butts[19] has explored what he calls the *unumpluribus* tension. In their analyses, the country has been through an emphasis upon individualism and pluralism. The country may now be shifting toward more unity (*unum*), which could mean some "condensing" of values. The general public may become increasingly sympathetic to a prevalence of Judeo-Christian values, as expressed in traditional values.

Given the diversity in American culture, Christians cannot expect to reinstitute distinctively Christian values as the single, or even dominant, moral direction in the public schools. They may be able to lobby for "traditional values" if they work in unprecedented unity among themselves and compromise with other religious and secular citizens with similar concerns about "values in education." A compromise for common ground through common grace is one that even the Puritans might approve.[20]

Chapter 4

THE MYTH
OF
NEUTRALITY

Richard A. Baer, Jr.

"Just teach the basics: reading, writing, and 'rithmetic." That's the solution some offer to avoid conflict over what values are taught in public schools. But can education be "value free" or "value neutral"? No, says Richard Baer of Cornell University. For even an act as simple as passing out papers—"Does everyone have one?"—assumes the value of fairness, that every child ought to have a paper.

And we are equally mistaken if we believe that avoiding the language and practice of organized religion guarantees a value-neutral environment. Any time schools touch upon what Baer calls the "Big Questions," they are dealing with matters important to religious faith.

In the following chapter, Baer traces how what was once labeled "nonsectarian" education became known as "secular" education, and how "secular" has come to be regarded as "value neutral." More than an exercise in semantics, such changes reflect society's assumptions about the role of religion and values in education. The result of this evolving language is disturbingly real: Discrimination against religious ideas and people is taking place in our schools.

The first step toward a solution, Baer writes, is a recognition of the problem.

America's government-owned, government-funded, government-run public schools are not religiously neutral today, nor have they ever been. Every school curriculum is based on fundamental religious or philosophical assumptions and commitments—values, if you will. And whenever public schools address the Big Questions—the meaning and purpose of life, the nature of the good life and of the good society—they enter the arena of religion.

Unfortunately, Horace Mann, a key figure in the founding of the compulsory common school, did not adequately appreciate the religious particularity of his own thinking. While he believed that effective education without moral and religious instruction was impossible, he insisted that only *nonsectarian* religion, based on reason, science, and common experience, would be appropriate for the common school. He was convinced that such rational religion stood in sharp contrast to the faith of Calvinists, Catholics, and other orthodox Christians. Their religion was dogmatic, superstitious, parochial, and *sectarian*; it did not belong in the public schools.

As most impartial critics today would easily grant, however, Mann's views were hardly religiously neutral, and thus it was not surprising that orthodox Christians of Mann's day opposed him. They rightly understood that Mann's so-called *nonsectarian* religion, which in fact was nearly identical to his own Unitarian faith, was no more neutral or nonsectarian than were their own beliefs. In the early 1840s, Catholic Bishop John Hughes clearly saw through the Unitarian bias of Mann's "nonsectarian" religion. In his argument with the Public School Society of New York, Hughes "clearly set forth the fundamental dilemma created by every effort to maintain a majoritarian, monopolistic, public school system in a religiously pluralist society. He pointed out that it was impossible for one group of Christians to teach the 'essentials of religion' without offending the beliefs of some other group. . . . And if it were assumed that religion could be eliminated from education, then students would be left 'to the advantage of infidelity.' "[1]

Their opposition, however, did not last long, for during the 1830s and 1840s suspicion and fear of growing numbers of Roman Catholic immigrants led many orthodox Protestants to give at least grudging support to Mann's version of the common school. Apparently, they preferred to endure the threat of Unitarian indoctrination in the common school, they reasoned, than to risk the more serious "contamination" of American and Protestant values and beliefs from the Catholic immigrants. Tragically, orthodox Protestants failed to realize they were theologically closer to the Catholics than to the Unitarians. (On this debate, see chapter 6, "A New Definition of 'Public' Education," by Rockne McCarthy.)

Horace Mann's *nonsectarian* religion was no new development. Indeed, it was similar to the faith of Thomas Jefferson, who, as is evident from his private correspondence, nurtured a lifelong bias against both clerics and orthodox Christianity. Presbyterians, Catholics, and all traditional Christians, according to Jefferson, based their religion on superstition, dogma, and revelation; it was parochial and *sectarian*. By contrast, Jefferson was convinced that his own moral and religious thinking was based on reason, science, and common sense; it was universal and *nonsectarian* and deserved to become the basis for the public life of the nation. Although a strong defender of religious freedom, Jefferson nonetheless believed that *sectarian* religion belonged at home and in the churches, not in public. Indeed, he fervently hoped that such traditional religion would gradually suffer "a quiet euthanasia" as Americans progressed toward greater enlightenment.[2]

The distinction made by Jefferson and Mann between a public nonsectarian religion and a private sectarian religion was by no means uncontroversial. Both thinkers shared the widespread Enlightenment conviction of their day that reason itself would lead to knowledge, not only in the natural sciences, but also in morality, political theory, and religion. Catholics and orthodox Protestants, however, continued to insist on the importance of revelation and the church for coming to a proper knowledge of God.

Today, few philosophers or theologians share Jefferson's or Mann's ebullient confidence in reason's power to determine truth in religion and morality. Orthodox theologians continue to stress the importance of revelation in coming to a full knowledge of God. And most nontheistic philosophers emphasize that human thinking rests on basic assumptions or intuitions; it is impossible to think without such initial commitments, or to doubt all of them at once. (This is not to imply, however, that such basic assumptions must be believed for no reason at all. The basic convictions of the Christian faith can be defended by reason, as can the basic assumptions that philosophers make. The point is that reason and experience simply do not provide the kind of certainty that Jefferson took for granted. All human knowing involves risk and uncertainty.)

From "nonsectarian" to "secular"
Because it is so closely related to public schools' current commitment to secular education, the dedication of Jefferson and Mann to what they termed nonsectarian education in the common school is of more than mere historical interest. Likewise, developing a clear understanding of the use and relationship of these terms is more than just an etymological exercise. For the problematic nature of our current attitude toward religion in public education is perhaps best illustrated by the terminology employed in public rhetoric.

By the early 1840s, the term *secular* began to be used as a synonym for *nonsectarian*. For example, in defending its educational views before the New York City Common Council, the Public School Society stated: "We have the right to declare moral truths. . . . We thus undertake in these public schools to furnish this *secular education*, embracing as it does, not solely and exclusively the common rudiments of learning, but also a knowledge of good morals, and those common sanctions of religion which are acknowledged by everybody."[3]

By the mid-twentieth century, the term *secular* had virtually replaced *nonsectarian*, thus obscuring the religious roots of the latter. And the notion that public schools offered a secular—meaning "nonreligious"—education was firmly established in the public's mind. At the same time, the term *sectarian* fell into similarly new, and troubling, usage.

Discrimination in high places
Over the past 40 years, in public discussion and in the courts—including the U.S. Supreme Court—the term *sectarian* has become a synonym for *religious*. This usage has become so common that the

Court now regularly refers to sectarian schools and colleges, sectarian curricula, sectarian purposes, and even to sectarian schoolchildren and school personnel.[4]

Given the enormous sensitivity of our society today to discriminatory language, however, such usage is really quite extraordinary. A quick reading of any dictionary will reveal that *sectarian* is associated with such terms as *narrow-minded, biased, bigoted, heretical, unorthodox,* and *schismatic.* While the Court doubtless does not intend to be pejorative in its use of the word, the effects are no less damaging. No profound social discernment is required to understand that when the highest tribunal of the land refers to religious Americans and their beliefs and values with the term *sectarian,* the Court is using a word that should be no more socially acceptable than the use of racial epithets in its decisions.

For the U.S. Supreme Court to use such language becomes particularly alarming when we recall that fundamental to the First Amendment and the American political experiment is the conviction that government has no right to determine what is orthodox or heretical in religion. The Court's use of *sectarian* and *nonsectarian* implies, albeit unintentionally, that religious Americans are not part of the mainstream, are not thinking correctly, are unorthodox and schismatic. By implying that there is a right way of thinking and living as Americans—namely the *nonsectarian* or *secular* way—government makes second-class citizens out of religious Americans and is clearly outside its realm of legitimacy and competence.

This is in no way to deny the fruitfulness of the political insight of the Founders that public strife could be avoided by excluding religious, and particularly denominational, language and views from most everyday public intercourse. As long as government limited its activities to matters such as harbor dredging, maintaining an army and navy, and running the postal service, such a nonreligious or secular mode was not highly controversial. It is, after all, hard even to imagine a distinctively Presbyterian form of bridge building, a Jewish style of post-office operation, or a Catholic method for operating toll roads. But when society becomes religiously more pluralistic, and when government expands into the fields of education and social welfare—areas of considerable concern for religion—such prudential limitations on language and style become unacceptable to many Americans, for it is not at all odd or inappropriate to think of a Catholic view of marriage and birth control, an Orthodox Jewish view of the family, or an evangelical Protestant view of divorce. Excluding religious language and values from public education and social welfare results in a de facto state endorsement of secular values and beliefs. It favors viewpoints that compete with religious understandings and values.

What, in effect, has happened during the past 40 years is that Jefferson's and Mann's bias against certain religious people and beliefs, mainly orthodox Christians and their faith, has been extended to religious people in general.

Textbook bias
Clarifying the meaning and use of the term *sectarian* should pave the way for a more objective, dispassionate—and, one hopes, just— analysis of religion in education today. Once it is understood that the term *sectarian* has always tended to make some Americans into second-class citizens; that there is little if any philosophical or theological justification for the way the term was used by Jefferson and Mann; and that the common school was oppressive to Jews, Catholics, atheists, and others throughout the first hundred years of its existence, as indeed history shows—once all this is understood, policy makers may be in a better position to take a clear-headed look at current school policy.

Such historical understanding may make it easier to listen to the protests of millions of Americans today who claim that government public schools are discriminatory and unjust. The evidence for such contemporary discrimination has been documented in detail in dozens of scholarly articles. This discrimination takes at least two forms.

First, we see bias in the curriculum. There are very specific, easily identifiable instances, such as Values Clarification, where school curricula have been laden with values that are oppressive for specific religious groups. Advertised as a neutral, noncoercive way to teach values by clarifying the student's own values rather than inculcating someone else's, Values Clarification actually indoctrinates students.

A number of scholars have pointed out that the method presses upon students particularistic and highly debatable views about the nature of morality and of human beings. Without any indication of how controversial such a position is or any discussion of alternatives, Values Clarification presupposes the fact of moral relativism and subjectivism—that is, the position that all value judgments are matters of personal preference and taste, and that there are no objective values that can be known to be true or false, right or wrong. Likewise, it encourages by its self-centered approach the belief that the purpose of life is to meet one's own needs and fulfill one's own desires, a position that contradicts and undermines the belief of Jews and Christians that human beings are meant to love God and serve one another (or the convictions of many nontheistic humanists that one should subordinate self-interest to the good of the total community).

The problem, however, is not a lack of sophisticated, scholarly analysis;[5] rather, the problem lies with school administrators who lack either the philosophical competence or the commitment to fairness and public justice to deal with the issue in a reasonable and just manner.

Many courses in sex education and home economics have also been shown to be filled with values that many Christians find objectionable. Expert witnesses in the 1986 Alabama textbook trial presented hundreds of pages of sophisticated analysis of the five home-economics textbooks used at that time in Alabama, pointing out scores of passages in conflict with traditional Christian understandings. As in the case of Values Clarification, the books presented a variety of nontheistic views of human nature and the meaning and purpose of human existence, and made no serious effort at all to balance these presentations with competing points of view. These textbooks regularly took positions that were biased against parents and against traditional religion and morality (and authority in general), and fostered a variety of highly debatable modern views of the nature of human beings and the purpose of life.

A second way in which curricula are value laden is through what might be called *a bias of omission*. Prof. Paul Vitz of New York University has documented in detail the extent to which public schools have discriminated against Christian values and beliefs by simply omitting them from consideration.[6] In some social studies textbooks such bias is so complete that it becomes virtually impossible for students to gain an appreciation of the vital role that religion has played in American culture.

The basis of curriculum

By eliminating Values Clarification and offensive aspects of sex-education curricula, schools could, in principle, devise programs less discriminatory towards religious and ideological minorities. It would also be possible to teach students about the important role that religion plays in American history and contemporary life.

However, the more basic hindrance to achieving true religious neutrality in schools is the fact that every school curriculum inevitably presupposes a particular understanding of human nature and of the good life, and for some students this orientation will be oppressive.

For example, take the case of a family committed to strong environmental values. Their consciences may demand that they live in a way that is far less competitive and consumption oriented than what is common in our society. They may adhere to a radically biocentric view of the world, a view in which human beings are morally obligated to live at peace with other creatures and leave as light an imprint on the land as possible. Parents in such a family might believe that it is essential for their children to learn a great deal about appreciation for nature, about careful stewardship of natural resources, and about aesthetics and ecology. They may believe it necessary to shield their children from a curriculum that is oriented toward economic success and the exploitation of nature, as indeed most public school curriculum is.

For such a family, or for Christian and Jewish and Muslim families who hold to other values out of harmony with public schools as they exist today, the school will be experienced as an oppressive institution, where the consciences of parents are violated by having to submit their children to an institution where their deeply-held values are regularly violated and compromised. Within our current public-school system, no obvious means is available to adjust the curriculum to satisfy the needs of such minorities.

In their justification of current educational policy, some nontheistic humanists continue to make the same fundamental mistake as

Jefferson and Mann. They believe that secular approaches to the Big Questions can be rational, scientific, and impartial.

But such thinkers need to realize that liberal reason has failed to deliver the goods. The Enlightenment's conviction that there is some kind of neutral process that will allow us to achieve purely rational answers to the Big Questions is a failed enterprise. Because of that failure, we must, if we are to be consistent, not only reject Jefferson's and Mann's thinking about the distinctive rationality of their own religious views, but also reject modern claims by secularists that their views of education and the good life can be considered religiously neutral.

Not only have the defenders of current education policy failed to realize that reason as such cannot give us clear and certain conclusions about the nature of the good life, but they have also operated with an unduly restrictive definition of the term *religion*, as has the Supreme Court in most cases dealing with the relationship between religion and education and the public life.

In *Seeger* v. *United States* and *Welsh* v. *United States*, two cases dealing with conscientious objection to military service, the Supreme Court broadened its definition of religion. It ruled that a deeply held, nontraditional religious belief or even a secular belief could constitute legitimate grounds for being granted conscientious objector status (even though the statutory law in question specifically required belief in a "Supreme Being").[7] The Court properly understood that an individual's conscience could be influenced by nontraditional religious beliefs or by secular beliefs, as well as by traditional religious beliefs. In these two cases, a broader definition of religion prevailed.

Unfortunately, in cases dealing with religion and education—and with virtually all First Amendment religious *establishment* cases—the Court regularly uses a narrower definition of religion, one that views religion mainly in terms of traditional theistic beliefs and practices.

It is this use of a restricted definition of religion that lies at the heart of our current predicament. For if a narrow definition of religion is used in cases dealing with religion and education, then, as was apparent from the recent Tennessee and Alabama textbook trials, religious Americans are left with an intolerable situation: The state must promulgate *no* traditional religious beliefs in its schools, but it is free to promulgate whatever nontheistic or even atheistic beliefs it chooses, for these are "nonreligious" or "nonsectarian." Thus, promoting them is not constitutionally prohibited.

To escape this dilemma, the Court must adopt *one* definition of religion—a broad *functional* definition—for all cases, both free exercise and establishment cases. It should recognize that the First Amendment's interest in religion is not mainly in bar mitzvahs, Communion services, baptisms, or church architecture. It is rather in how religion *functions as the bearer of ultimate meaning*. Religion is to be protected because of our utterly basic commitment as Americans to safeguard the freedom of each other's consciences—not in the frivolous sense of permitting individuals to choose whatever their momentary passions and desires dictate, but in the sense of being free to act upon their deepest convictions about who they are and how they ought to conduct their lives—consistent, of course, with the similar freedom of others.

Within the context of a functional definition of religion, it is just as improper for the state to promulgate nontheistic or secular humanistic answers to the Big Questions—such as those that underlie Values Clarification or sex education curricula—as it is for it to recommend traditional Christian or Jewish beliefs. The claim that secular humanism is not a religion is wrong. It is essential to discredit this claim if we are to achieve justice in public education.

This is not to say that every wild pronouncement about secular humanism and moral relativism should be taken seriously. Made on occasion by well-known Christian leaders, such claims have degraded public rhetoric concerning religion and education. Still, it is essential to recall that John Dewey and a whole generation of nontheistic humanists maintained that their nontheistic beliefs were "religious." Only in our day, when this claim has been seen to carry with it certain obligations as well as privileges, has it been dropped and discounted by most nontheistic humanists.

Policy alternatives
No policy that ignores the monopolistic character of our system of school finance can achieve justice in public education. At present, only government public schools have full access to public tax

monies. Families who experience these schools as oppressive have no choice but to continue to pay for this system and then, if they are able, to pay for their children's education in an alternative school. As Stephen Arons writes in his book *Compelling Belief,* we have in America "a system of school finance that provides free choice for the rich and compulsory socialization for everyone else."[8]

It is this monopolistic aspect of American education that is most troubling in terms of freedom of conscience. Until society makes it economically possible for those who conscientiously object to the system to send their children to alternative schools without economic hardship, the system will remain unjust.

Defenders of the status quo typically have refused to support various voucher or tax-credit proposals. Failing to understand the religious nonneutrality of the schools, many educators remain blind even to the existence of government discrimination against minorities of conscience. Others, aware of such discrimination, believe that the risk of social fragmentation resulting from a voucher system outweighs the problems that currently exist.

Conceivably, public schools could decide not to deal with the Big Questions at all, and limit the curriculum to the transmission of information and technical skills. But such a move seems unlikely in the extreme, and even if it were made it would, in itself, constitute taking a position vis-à-vis the Big Questions: namely, that we live in the kind of world where education can proceed satisfactorily without considering them openly and explicitly.

Another strategy would be to incorporate greater diversity into the curriculum and to teach more about religion. The Christian Legal Society and the National Association of Evangelicals gave their support in 1988 to a two-page statement entitled *Religion in the Public School Curriculum: Questions and Answers,*[9] a short paper aimed at school board members and administrators, which emphasizes objective teaching about religion in public schools in ways that are constitutionally permissible.

Such an approach, however, does not adequately consider the fact that a comparative and "objective" approach to the study of religion may very well produce in students, particularly younger students, a more relativistic understanding of the truth of their own religious heritage. And if such courses are taught by religious skeptics, they may tend to undermine rather than encourage personal faith. Also, by failing to admit that nontheistic, humanistic values and beliefs can function as religion, the document accepts severe restrictions on how traditional religion may be dealt with in public schools, but utterly fails to place limits on the promulgation of nontheistic beliefs and values.

For government to get out of the business of public education altogether—other than funding it and defining in minimal terms the state's compelling interest in an educated citizenry—might in the long run lead to the highest degree of public justice in education. However, the chances of our society making such a move in the near future are practically nil.

The struggle for change
Those who want to change the system, therefore, might more realistically act on three fronts: (1) attempt to educate fellow Americans about the high degree of discrimination toward religious and ideological minorities that currently exists in government public schools; (2) demand that greater diversity be incorporated into the present system and that current censorship of religious values and points of view be ended; (3) work for a system of educational funding that would enable families who conscientiously object to the present system to send their children to alternative schools without economic hardship. Such a system would have to prohibit any kind of racial discrimination and, ideally, be designed in such a manner that poor families would be able to compete with well-to-do families for top-quality education for their children.

Such an overhaul of the present system—even granting that it might lead to more efficient as well as just schools—will not come quickly or without a great deal of struggle. In the meantime, Christians, Jews, and other religious people might well consider mounting a campaign to persuade government, including our courts, to cease using the term *sectarian* as a synonym for *religious*. Such a limited goal is achievable, is just, and would elevate the public rhetoric to a new level of fairness. Achieving one such specific victory would send a strong message to all those concerned about the issue of religion and public life that religious Americans are not willing to acquiesce to the status of second-class citizenship.

CHANGING THE SYSTEM

Chapter 5

THE OPEN DOOR OF SCHOOL REFORM

Charles L. Glenn

One component of many current school-reform measures is parental choice—an approach to public education that allows parents to pick the school they wish their children to attend. Rather than students being automatically assigned to a school according to their home address, they can choose from a variety of options, such as high quality "magnet" schools, those with a special emphasis on languages, science, or the arts.

With this choice comes greater opportunity for parents and concerned citizens to shape the schools in their communities not only in structure and programming, but in the values and character they wish those schools to nurture. Such opportunity, writes Charles Glenn, executive director of the Office of Educational Equity for the Massa-

chusetts Department of Education, is an open door for concerned Christians to effect positive change in the moral climate of public education. Combined with other elements of the current reform movement, such as the growing awareness of the need for character formation and appreciation of the role of religion in American life and history, this opportunity for involvement makes it possible for Christians to restore the moral climate they feel has been lost in public education.

C hristians concerned about public schools—and surely, in some sense, that includes all of us—can take encouragement from several recent developments. No, public education has not changed overnight. But policy makers and opinion shapers are rethinking what needs to change. In the past several years, the ground has shifted more dramatically than at any time in the quarter-century that I have been involved in education policy debates.

There is nothing new about demands for educational reform; they are a recurring theme in American history. But there is a sense of urgency about reform now, and that urgency is accompanied by a shift in the *focus* of demands for reform.

The new focus goes beyond concern about methods of teaching or asking whether teachers are well enough paid or trained. The new focus raises questions about the institution of public schooling itself. No longer do Americans give unquestioning support to public schools "in the firm belief that they are the ark of the national salvation," as a businessman wrote a century ago.

The publication of the national report *A Nation at Risk* in April 1983 set an apocalyptic tone with its celebrated words,

> If an unfriendly foreign power had attempted to impose on America the mediocre educational performance that exists today, we might well have viewed it as an act of war. As it stands, we have allowed this to happen to ourselves. . . . Our society and its educational institutions seem to have lost sight of the basic purposes of schooling, and of the high expectations and disciplined effort needed to attain them.[1]

A Nation at Risk was followed by a flood of reports on different aspects of the educational performance crisis. It also stimulated new mandates by state legislatures—since it is the states and not the federal government that control American education—to raise expectations and require disciplined effort. New course requirements, testing programs, and standards for teacher competency were written into law across the country.

Much of this effort, by making a clear statement about what society expects of schools, was salutary. Yet the basic problems faced by public schools were only compounded by the side effects of these programs and requirements. They stumbled into the same bureaucratic black hole that has swallowed up many past educational reforms. Why have past reforms had so little lasting effect? Because, many believe, the very structure of American public education has a way of absorbing new challenges and turning them into paperwork, of turning the delicate art of nurturing a child's mind into routines and busywork.

Recent discussion has increasingly focused on the need for fundamental changes in this structure. A useful analogy may be the current reform efforts in the Soviet Union. Decades of attempts to stimulate the Soviet economy through top-down mandates, with detailed requirements, have produced a stagnating system. Western observers agree that basic structural changes, the *perestroika* sought by Mikhail Gorbachev, are needed. To be effective, such changes must free the system and the individuals whose energy and commitment have been stifled by the "command economy" of the past; these changes must place decision-making responsibility at the level where the decisions' effects are apparent.

Multinational corporations have learned the same lessons: It is self-defeating to centralize nonstrategic decision making; an open system in which people are free to experiment, react to new situations, and even make mistakes is far more effective.

American public education is beginning to learn this lesson as well. Top-down decisions and detailed attempts to regulate the classroom do not result in effective schools. They may produce some immediate results, but the long-term effect is stagnation.

Perhaps the most powerful case for such restructuring was made in a May 1986 report prepared for the Carnegie Forum on Education and the Economy, *A Nation Prepared*. The report called for "a new framework" for teaching:

> Bureaucratic management of schools proceeds from the
> view that teachers lack the talent or motivation to think for

themselves. . . . Within the context of a limited set of clear goals for students set by state and local policymakers, teachers, working together, must be free to exercise their professional judgment as to the best way to achieve these goals.[2]

This logic was taken a step further in an August 1986 report by the National Governors' Association, *Time for Results*, in which chairman Lamar Alexander of Tennessee announced that "the Governors are ready for some old-fashioned horse-trading. We'll regulate less, if schools and school districts will produce better results."[3]

This offer was a clear reversal from the initial response to *A Nation at Risk*, a great increase in state regulation of schools. The governors' offer recognized the need to give teachers more freedom—and accountability—to teach effectively, and it also recognized that parents had to be empowered to assure that this freedom was used in ways that matched their own goals for their children. As the governors pointed out, the

changes will require more rewards for success and consequences for failure for teachers, school leaders, schools, and school districts. It will mean giving parents more choice of the public schools their children attend as one way of assuring higher quality without heavy-handed state control.[4]

As Governor Richard Lamm of Colorado added, the recent school-reform efforts had failed to look critically at the system itself. The governors hoped

that in ten years the country does not look back and find that we kicked up a lot of dust and then settled for business as usual. We propose something in the great American tradition: that you increase excellence by increasing the choices. . . . A more responsive system would incorporate what students and their parents say they need with the education services necessary to meet it.[5]

A concern for higher standards, then, has led to a conviction that it is essential to restructure public education to give responsibility—and the freedom that must go with it—to those working directly with students. This freedom to teach requires that public schools be encouraged to become more diverse, more distinctive, each with a coherent educational mission. Increased parental choice can make this possible by assuring that each school will be able to focus on satisfying some parents very much rather than seeking not to offend any.

These, then, are issues that current school-reform discussions focus upon: higher standards, professional autonomy, school distinctiveness, and parental choice. They reinforce one another, and together they add up to a call for fundamental structural change in American public education.

The challenge of change
Such change will not come easily. The "education establishment" is divided on whether to support such fundamental change. Those pressing for it tend to be political and business leaders who have no stake in the present system. Thus a book published in early 1988 by David Kearns, the chairman and CEO of the Xerox Corporation, and education consultant Denis Doyle, *Winning the Brain Race*, argued that "today's educational system is a failed monopoly." They called for "a new education marketplace fueled by academic diversity and free choice."[6]

Although change will not come overnight, it is coming. For several years now Albert Shanker, the powerful president of the American Federation of Teachers, has been calling for basic restructuring, including more opportunity for parental choice. In many states—including my own Massachusetts—there are new political initiatives in the same direction, almost always coming from non-educators.

Consider, for example, one issue that would reflect increased parental choice, the issue of educational vouchers. A recent national Gallup poll found that 49 percent of potential voters said they would be more likely to vote for a presidential candidate who supported giving parents educational vouchers to pay public or private school tuition through tax money, compared with 27 percent who would be less likely to do so. The two groups most supportive of vouchers, the survey found, were socially conservative Republicans (54 percent) and low-income Democrats who support more social spending (62 percent).[7]

There has always been parental choice in the United States, of course, provided parents were prepared to pay for it. In most of the Western democracies—Canada, Great Britain, Australia, West Germany, France, and others—public funds are provided to Catholic, Protestant, and Jewish schools on the basis of their enrollment. This is not likely to happen here unless the Supreme Court reverses the tendency of postwar interpretations of the First Amendment regarding separation of church and state.

The current policy debates, then, center on whether alternatives should be deliberately developed within public education in response to the different ways in which teachers want to teach and in which parents want their children to learn. This trend in school reform will provide many opportunities for Christians to have an influence on public schools, and to do so in a way that is consistent with religious freedom.

In the past, most decisions have been made at the level of superintendents and elected school boards, and Christians with concerns about the schools have been put in the position of going over the heads of teachers and principals to seek to have policies changed or instructions issued to every school. It is no wonder that such efforts received a bad press. The widespread perception has been that groups within the community were attempting to impose their morality or beliefs upon the children of others, and that the "academic freedom" of teachers was being threatened.

In top-down school systems, of course, academic freedom is a joke. But there was enough truth in these criticisms to arouse political and legal opposition. Vocal Christian parents acquired an undeserved reputation as "book burners," a reputation that has made it extremely difficult for any kind of productive dialogue and give-and-take to occur.

As the trend toward school-level autonomy and choice continues, however, it will become possible to develop instructional goals and disciplinary policies affecting only one school and only those people who have been involved in the goal- and policy-making process. Parents, teachers, and secondary students will buy into results they themselves have helped to shape; or they will be free to seek another school whose mission they can support wholeheartedly.

Of course, in the American legal context, this process will not produce explicitly Christian schools. But it could well create schools that reflect communities of shared values, schools in which the grayness of "defensive teaching" is replaced by the rich colors of teaching based upon convictions about the purpose of education. Teachers who know they are supported by parents, parents who trust what the teachers represent, students who know that their parents and teachers are in accord—these add up to a good education.

For example, an exciting development in Massachusetts education has been a growing partnership of parents and teachers around many of the 140 public schools that enroll their students by choice. Three of my own children are in a Boston elementary school whose theme is that all its students learn in both English and Spanish. Teachers have been cautious about applying the theme of the school consistently and perhaps demanding too much of the children; it has been the parents who have pressed them to be bolder in making the school distinctive. Now a dozen other schools across the state are implementing similar programs with strong support from parents.

We have similar "magnet" schools whose unifying theme is an approach to character development and discipline. Interestingly, those that announce a child-centered or "discovery" (to use the jargon) approach to values have been developed more consistently than schools that teach and encourage students to practice the traditional virtues. I believe this is because many parents who are strong and articulate supporters of the second approach have withdrawn their children from the public schools, usually in favor of private Christian schools, while others who would favor it are predisposed to accept the authority of the school without their own active involvement. This is a shame. It reduces the diversity possible within public education and weakens the ties of many parents to the education and development of their children.

Many public schools have become morally incoherent—incapable of developing any consistent character—out of a fear of offending some parent and thus causing controversy. This is a more substantial problem than an imagined conspiracy to promote "secular humanism." Those who see such a conspiracy give too much credit to an educational system that (for all the high character and ideals of many teachers and administrators) is singularly mindless and waffling when it comes to questions of moral purpose.

Discouraging experiences with such schools in the past may have produced withdrawal or passivity in many parents. But this should not prevent them from taking advantage of the opportunities created by today's new emphasis on school-level diversity and parent and teacher choice. It will be increasingly possible for parents to work together with a group of like-minded teachers to develop a public school with a distinctive flavor, one that would not be acceptable to every parent or teacher, but highly satisfactory to some. That is part of the promise held out by the new stress on the structural reform of public education.

A precious inheritance

Although I have stressed structural reforms, two current emphases in the area of curriculum are important to Christian parents.

One is a rediscovery of the importance of developing character and civic virtue. If there is any concern central to parents, it is this one. Unfortunately, since the 1960s educators have resisted accepting responsibility for it. This may be changing. In 1987, for example, a broad-based group of educational leaders, including the presidents of the two major teachers' unions, issued a *Statement of Principles* on "education for democracy." They concluded that "we are part of the noblest political effort in history. Our children must learn, and we must teach them, the knowledge, values, and habits that will best protect and extend this precious inheritance."[8]

This is worlds away from the premise behind values clarification—that students should be encouraged to decide for themselves which values to accept, with their teachers serving only as coaches to help them confront the issues. Christian parents will welcome the change, but they will want to work closely with teachers to assure that the approaches used are consistent with their own convictions.

A second emphasis in discussions of curriculum is the need to do more justice to the role of religion in American life. It is generally recognized on all sides now that students have been given a distorted picture of a world in which religion figures, if at all, as a quaint survival of an earlier age. As the Williamsburg Charter, adopted in July 1988, noted, our society has moved recently

> toward the de facto semi-establishment of a wholly secular understanding of the origin, nature and destiny of human-kind and of the American nation. During this period, the exclusion of teaching about the role of religion in society, based partly upon a misunderstanding of First Amendment decisions, has ironically resulted in giving a dominant status to such wholly secular understandings. . . .[9]

In response to the growing recognition that this represents an impoverished framework for education, textbooks are being rewritten and supplementary classroom materials are being prepared, and we can expect to see more attention to America's religious traditions and communities in teacher-training programs.

Christian parents should welcome this—but with some caution. Some who are calling for more teaching about religion overemphasize the dangers of religious persecution. Religious liberty is, of course, an important part of our heritage. But the story can be told so that the religious beliefs of the majority are presented as a perpetual threat to those—always the heroes of the account—who dare to question them. The end result is to devalue traditional belief and to make rejecting it seem glamorous.

In both of these curriculum areas, the new stress on school-level autonomy and opportunities for parents to choose schools best matching their own educational goals will provide many opportunities for cooperation between parents and teachers. Increasingly, parental concerns will be heard and accommodated without confrontation and bitterness.

The pace of change may be slow. Public education has not traditionally encouraged teachers and principals to break away from the herd and create distinctive schools. For all the lip service given to parental involvement, this has seldom meant helping to define the mission of the school and how that will be lived out in daily practice. New habits will have to develop over time.

But parents who are concerned about the experience of their children in public schools should be encouraged by the direction in which the educational debate is moving. They should be aware that the messages received by educators from the publications they read and the conferences they attend are bringing home the need to become more open, flexible, daring, and responsive to parental concerns.

Educational reform is taking a direction that will make it possible to bridge the gap that has grown between public schools and many Christian parents.

The views expressed here are personal opinions of the author and are not intended to reflect those of the Massachusetts Board of Education.

Chapter 6

A NEW DEFINITION OF "PUBLIC" EDUCATION

Rockne M. McCarthy

What makes a public school public? Is it the source of its money, or the service it performs? In this chapter, Rockne McCarthy, dean of social sciences at Dordt College, explores the answers—and calls for a new direction in the structuring of public education.

The government-owned, -managed, and -financed schools that we regard today as public education, McCarthy argues, are in fact the product of the self-serving interests of a nineteenth-century Protestant majority. Based on the faulty assumption that a secular education can be value neutral, public schools fail to serve the plurality of beliefs found today in our country. And they virtually exclude Christian concerns.

Mere adjustments in the current system are not enough, according to McCarthy. Its ideology and structure are inherently unjust. What is the solution? A new definition of public education which produces schools that serve the public good by providing quality education, whether they be publicly funded, privately run, or church sponsored. Just as the ecclesiastical monopoly was disestablished in the eighteenth century, so too must the current educational monopoly be disestablished. Only then, in a truly pluralistic system of education, will values be freely taught and encouraged.

I n the present national controversy over moral education in public schools, there is no consensus on how Christians ought to respond. Scripture does, however, suggest two areas of responsibility for Christians. First, as parents, we have a responsibility to educate our children in a manner that supports and deepens a biblical view of life. At the same time, Scripture places upon us a second responsibility: as Christian citizens, we take seriously the biblical principle of public justice. This includes a commitment to protecting parents' freedom to provide an education for their children that does not contradict home-taught values and perspectives on life.

Both of these responsibilities flow from the biblical teaching that Christ is Lord over every aspect and activity of life. There can be no such thing for the Christian, therefore, as value-free or value-neutral education. Nor can Christians work in public education and politics in any way other than that which strengthens rather than undermines our pluralist, democratic society.

The problem now, however, is that a *nonpluralist* understanding of public education keeps Christian parents and Christian citizens from fulfilling their educational responsibility to their children and their fellow citizens. This is because public education today is defined to include only *secular* schools that are government owned, managed, and funded. This narrow view of public education results in an educational monopoly that does not represent the diversity of values and educational viewpoints in our contemporary society.[1]

The nineteenth-century "establishment"
This understanding of "public" education emerged in the middle of the nineteenth century. Before this time there was no clean line separating a public from a private school.[2]

In New York City, for example, the division occurred as a result of a bitter controversy between supporters of the New York Public School Society, a private corporation that had gained a monopoly of public funds for its schools, and supporters of Catholic schools in the city.[3] By 1840, large-scale immigration of Irish Catholics to New York produced a significant ethnic community with its own newspapers, social clubs, schools, and professional elites. These Catholics refused to send their children to the society's schools, which clearly reflected a Protestant view, claiming instead a proportion of New York's common-school fund to support Catholic schools. The Roman Catholic Church had established seven Catholic schools in the city, open to all students, with more than 5,000 enrolled.

In a written petition to the Common Council of New York City, Bishop John Hughes argued that a private corporation having as one of its goals the "early religious instruction" of children controlled all funds for education.[4] In his oral presentation before the council, Hughes pointed out the bias against Catholics in this religious training. The bishop stressed that Catholics resented the violation of their children's religious conscience. They did not object to all groups sharing in the common-school fund; they objected only to the monopoly of the Public School Society.

Supporters of the Public School Society rejected Hughes's charge that the society's schools engaged in offensive, sectarian education. They stressed that their schools taught only the *universal* principles of virtue and morality. This was deemed the legitimate responsibility of common schools such as those run by the Public School Society.

In this nineteenth-century debate, each side was speaking past the other. Each rested its argument on a different understanding of religion. Hughes defined religion *holistically*. From his perspective, nonsectarian education was impossible, because education always reflects the world-and-life view of particular individuals and groups in society. Every effort to appeal to so-called universal or neutral moral precepts was merely an attempt to disguise a sectarian point of view. (For more on this question, see chapter 4, "The Myth of Neutrality.")

Supporters of the society's schools understood religion *dualistically*. To them the general core of moral principles differed from the specific doctrinal beliefs of the denominations, and thus one could teach universal principles of virtue and morality in a nonsectarian way.

Both sides failed to recognize their own religious presuppositions.

The bishop argued that one group could not teach morality without offending some other group, because individuals and groups will always differ regarding what moral education should be. His opponents could not comprehend this argument. Like Thomas Jefferson before them, and Horace Mann in their own day, they believed it was possible to foster universal moral training in a nonsectarian and nonoffensive way.[5]

In the end, the common council rejected the Catholic petition and the society continued to receive all the money from the common-school fund to support its schools. But the matter did not end here. Soon the New York State Senate became embroiled in the educational controversy. John C. Spencer, the New York secretary of state, acting in his capacity as *ex officio* superintendent of public schools, submitted in 1841 an official report to the state senate.

Spencer believed the state had legitimate interest in educating all children, because citizens must be educated to participate in the democratic process. But he was also concerned that the state's interest should be met without sacrificing the rights of any individual or group in society. He was careful to point out that "no books can be found, no reading lessons can be selected, which do not contain more or less of some principles of religious faith, either directly avowed, or indirectly assumed."[6] He applied this point directly to the activities of the Public School Society:

> Even the moderate degree of religious instruction which the Public School Society imparts, must therefore be sectarian; that is, it must favor one set of opinions in opposition to another, or others; *and it is believed that this always will be the result, in any course of education that the wit of man can devise.*[7]

As if to anticipate the modern argument about the possibility of secular education, Spencer pointed out that it was impossible to avoid sectarianism by abolishing religious instruction altogether:

> On the contrary, *it would be in itself sectarian;* because it would be consonant to the views of a peculiar class, and opposed to the opinions of other classes. Those who reject

creeds and resist all efforts to infuse them into the minds of the young before they have arrived at a maturity of judgment which may enable them to form their own opinions, would be gratified by a system which so fully accomplishes their purposes. But there are those who hold contrary opinions; and who insist on guarding the young against the influences of their own passions, and the contagion of vice, by implanting in their minds and hearts, those elements of faith which are held by this class to be the indispensable foundations of moral principles. This description of persons regards neutrality and indifference as the most insidious forms of hostility. It is not the business of the undersigned [John C. Spencer] to express any opinion on the merits of these views. *His only purpose is to show the mistake of those who suppose they may avoid sectarianism by avoiding all religious instruction.*[8]

Spencer went to the heart of the educational controversy by pointing out that calling something nonsectarian or neutral does not make it so. What is nonsectarian/neutral to one group is sectarian/nonneutral to another, because in education, ideas matter; education always reflects different views of life and different understandings of moral training. It is impossible to avoid sectarian or religious issues in education.

The question Spencer faced was how to allocate public funds to schools justly. He concluded that justice demanded he recognize "the choice of parents" in educating their children,[9] by distributing public funds to all schools, regardless of their perspectives on education.[10]

Spencer did not convince the New York State legislature of the justice of this position. In the face of growing anti-Catholic sentiment, any hope that a Protestant majority would approve educational funds going to a Catholic minority was out of the question. The best that could be accomplished was for the city to take over the schools of the Public School Society and place them under the supervision of an elected board of education and state superintendent of public schools.

This political development formalized a clean line of separation between public and private schools. The modern meaning of public education clearly reflects nineteenth-century political and ideological choices that were less self-evident than they were self-serving. Majoritarian interest self-consciously created a *nonpluralist educational monopoly* to exclude minorities from receiving public funds for their schools.

If we are to address adequately the issues involved in the present national controversy over moral education in public schools, we must recognize that an ideology of secular/religious and public/private separation, framed in the middle of the nineteenth century, defines the modern relationship between government and schools. The public schools in this country are organized on the premise that secular education can be isolated from all religious teaching, so that the school can inculcate all needed temporal knowledge and maintain a strict and lofty neutrality as to religion. The assumption is that after individuals are instructed in worldly wisdom, they will be better fitted to choose their religion.[11]

Fortunately, more and more persons are coming to realize that such a viewpoint regarding religion, education, and public life is *not* a value-neutral or self-evident assumption. Rather, it reflects a religious, philosophical ideology that has not been adequately recognized as such. It has created more problems than it has resolved in the continuing debate over majority and minority rights with respect to educational freedom. To support this ideology uncritically is to continue to uphold the legal fiction that schooling and public life can be value neutral.

Toward genuine educational pluralism and disestablishment
We have set ourselves the difficult task of supporting a monopolistic structure for public education that is to be at once capable of nurturing character and civic virtue and yet inoffensive to the convictions of minorities. Just how difficult this task is becomes evident when one analyzes the 1988 report *American Education: Making It Work*. It was issued by William Bennett, then U.S. secretary of education, on the fifth anniversary of the widely publicized report *A Nation at Risk*. One of the recommendations of this 1983 report was that in order to meet the crisis in American education, all high-school students must be required to take basic courses in

English, mathematics, science, social studies, and computer science for a specific number of years.

Five years after the publication of *A Nation at Risk*, Bennett reported that undeniable progress had been made in the number of students taking most of the "New Basics." But the secretary also pointed out that as a nation we are still at risk: "Student achievement has not kept pace with improved patterns in course-taking."[12] *Making It Work* makes clear that it is now "important to concentrate not just on which subjects our students study, but on the *actual content* of the courses they take."[13]

What Bennett's report suggests is that "we want our students—whatever their plans for the future—to take from high school a shared body of knowledge and skills, a common language of ideas, and a common moral and intellectual discipline.... We want them to develop, through example and experience, those habits of mind and traits of character properly prized by our society."[14]

To Bennett's credit he addressed such critical questions as "Whose values will be taught?" and "How?" These are the questions immediately asked when the "blending of character and ethics with knowledge and skills" is made the goal of education.[15] Bennett believes there are answers to these questions, and that there is a consensus about the kinds of character and ethics the American people want to instill as we implement this second phase of educational reform. But at what level, we might ask, does this national consensus exist? Is it possible to teach "character and ethics" meaningfully and effectively without making it clear to students by what standards or upon what authority morality and values rest? For education to be truly meaningful, teachers must be free not only to pose these questions, but to answer them as well. Not to answer them with conviction—in words and in actions—is to communicate a relativist world view.

Because it is virtually impossible to teach in such an authoritative way within the present meaning and structure of public education (secular schools that are exclusively government owned, managed, and funded), we must adopt a broader meaning and different structure. We must work to disestablish the present educational establishment and to create a more pluralist system—one in which there is equality for the plurality of educational viewpoints.

Perhaps the closest analogy to the present public-school establishment in our country is the state-church establishment of former days. As recently as the eighteenth century in America, for example, most people believed that one of the primary functions of an established church was to *enforce* a common morality. They assumed an ecclesiastical establishment was crucial to the very survival of society.

It is also clear that the first Americans who objected to the state-church establishment found it difficult to oppose because no society had as yet disestablished the church. When disestablishment finally did occur, people saw that a democratic society could indeed survive without one church having a favored political status.

Today many individuals and groups believe that disestablishing the public-school monopoly would threaten the survival of our society. We have, however, abundant evidence to demonstrate that democratic societies do not merely survive but flourish when a state recognizes a diversity of schools as legitimately fulfilling the task of educating young women and men for responsible citizenship.[16] It is curious that while the United States pointed the way for other democratic states to disestablish the church, it finds itself one of the few democratic countries in which a monopolistic education establishment is still maintained.

In the field of education, the rule of law and justice for all demands the nondiscriminatory allocation of educational resources to all citizens. The present efforts to offer greater freedom of choice to parents within the existing monopolistic structure of public education ought to be supported as a step toward recognizing parental choice as a basic right.

We often hear the argument that parents who object to what is taught in the present monopolistic structure can always have recourse to independent schools. But does this not make the exercise of conscience and of parental and institutional rights contingent upon the ability to afford an independent school?[17] Parental choice limited to the present, narrow meaning and monopolistic structure of public education fails to measure up to a truly democratic understanding of the rule of law and justice for all. To continue on the present nonpluralistic path will result in a never-ending controversy over moral education in public schools.

For the public good

Structurally speaking, the process whereby the church was disestablished in America ought to be followed in education. This does not mean it is necessary to prohibit the state from running any school system whatsoever; the only requirement is that true equity—proportional justice—must be instituted for all schools. In other words, funding provisions and all other public legal measures must be nondiscriminatory. No favor or penalty ought to be directed toward any particular school or school system.

Currently, there is little consensus among educators, researchers, and public-policy makers on whether *sponsorship* or educational *service* is a more relevant criterion for referring to a school as a public or private institution.[18] I am convinced that educational service is the more appropriate; therefore, the traditional contrast between public and private education should be dropped in favor of a contrast that avoids applying the term *public* to any one type of school. If distinctions are necessary for identification purposes, government and independent schools seems to be a good choice.

Of course, some still hold to the belief that the monopolistic government-sponsored school system provides the greater amount of public good and produces the highest level of social welfare. Whether or not this judgment is accurate depends upon whether or not one views diversity as something that contributes toward the public good. American pluralism and American education represent many perspectives. The question to be faced is this: Do the many perspectives inevitably lead to conflict and the undermining of the public good, or is diversity something to be accepted as a reality of American life and looked upon as the possible source of national richness and strength?

American pluralism is now so strong that the legitimate concern for a common unity will not come from attempts to overcome diversity; rather, respect for distinctiveness must be at the core of a common vision for the common good. Principled pluralism, the emphasis upon unity in the *interest* of diversity and not unity at the *expense* of diversity, must be reaffirmed as the original vision for our nation.[19]

Such was the vision expressed in the opening words of the Preamble to the Constitution: "We the people of the United States, in order to form a more perfect union, establish justice. . . ." This close linking of political unity with justice is a clear testimony that the framers felt the new country could not be based on common descent, religion, or language, but on the rule of law. Is it not the case that lasting, democratic unity proceeds from the bottom up, rather than from the top down? And is it not also true that the most effective democratic way of building up the public good among a pluralistic people is by administering the rule of law in such a way that genuine equity and justice is done toward "the many different perspectives and faces" that is America?

In this respect, the suggestion that educational *service* should be the criterion for judging the public character of schools is important. If we accept the argument that a common vision for the common good must be one that emphasizes unity in the interest of diversity, rather than unity at the expense of diversity, we should not limit our understanding of public education to government schools.

Educational research and experience is clearly demonstrating the significant public contribution that a wide variety of schools is making to American education and our democratic society.[20] It is clear that a government school is only one type of school that is providing a public service. The real distinction with respect to the concept of *public*, therefore, should be a distinction between public schools that are government sponsored, and public schools that are independently managed.

In the field of education, it is worth noting that before the creation of the monopolistic structure for public education that we have discussed, the criterion of educational service, not sponsorship, determined the meaning of public education. As Bernard Bailyn's insightful study of American educational history reveals, the "modern conception of public education, the very idea of a clean line of separation between 'private' and 'public,' was unknown before the end of the eighteenth century."[21] He further demonstrates that although the terms *public* and *private* were used to describe schools in the early national period, they referred only to the management of schools. Independent pay schools, academies, and denominational schools, for example, were often called *public schools* because they were understood to serve the public interest by preparing students for responsible public life, and the community stood to benefit if students attended the school of their choice.[22] In the early nineteenth century, few sharp lines between public and private education existed because *public* implied performance of broad social functions.

In American education today, more than ever before, we need to recognize the public contribution that a diversity of schools is making to the promotion of the public good. It is necessary to develop a broader political and legal definition of public education that includes all schools that are providing a public service by educating American youth in a professional and nondiscriminatory way. All parents who send their children to such schools should receive public funds. Only those schools that do not desire to be considered public schools, or do not wish to be judged by accreditation standards, would then be known as private schools.

When educational reform leads to the disestablishment of the present monopolistic structure of public education, Christian parents and Christian citizens will be better able to fulfill their educational responsibility to their children and their fellow citizens.

Chapter 7

WHO PAYS THE PRICE FOR SCHOOL REFORM?

Cliff Schimmels

The response to the current crisis in education has been to stiffen academic standards, raise test scores, and increase graduation requirements. However, Cliff Schimmels, professor of education at Wheaton College, believes some important questions have been ignored. While teachers, systems, bureaucracies, and funding have all been scrutinized, Schimmels asks, What effects are reforms having on students? *and,* What messages are the current reform measures sending to students with respect to values?

Schimmels observes that reform movements have come and gone. Their causes have varied, their results have been mixed and often fleeting. But in all of them, students have paid a certain price for reform.

An unabashed admirer of the contemporary student, the 52-year-old educator once spent six weeks enrolled as an "undercover" high-school freshman. Dubbed "the old guy" and accepted without second thought by his teenage classmates, Schimmels accompanied them through a daily schedule of classes, lunch breaks, and gym workouts. He came away from this experience with a profound respect for students' ability to survive the rigors of secondary education. But he fears that the increased pressure and competition created by many reform measures are communicating values Christians ought to consider. The time has come, Schimmels says, to think twice about the most important component of public education: the student.

School reform is not a new idea. It was what the Sophists had in mind when they came to Athens about 450 years before Christ was born. It was what the Roman emperor Justinian did when he banned pagan schools from the empire in A.D. 529. School reform was one element of the Lutheran Reformation; it was the entire thrust of the Jesuits during the Counter Reformation. And it was the consuming goal of more contemporary educational philosophers, such as Horace Mann and John Dewey.

Although each era was different, and each movement specific to its own period, school-reform movements throughout history have followed a similar pattern. First, some kind of national "crisis" sparks introspection and evaluation not only of schools, but of other social institutions. After much debate, the politicians decide that the root of the crisis is that children are not learning enough in school. This conclusion is followed by hasty and drastic changes in the educational system.

After a few urgent years of emergency reform, the crisis subsides, and schools go back to being pretty much what they were before the crisis. A mere residue of the reform ideas clings to the system.

Second place in space
As we examine this country's current reform movement—and try to anticipate where it will leave us in five or ten years—we would do well to learn from previous experience. The last round of school reform in the U.S. began in the early 1960s, with help from the Soviet Union. It provided the crisis in 1957 by launching the first spaceship, *Sputnik*. Suddenly we Americans found ourselves in second place.

In the early 1980s, the national crisis that called us to school reform was not quite so obvious. The best we could come up with was that the Japanese were building better automobiles.

The second step of the cycle, introspection and evaluation, has also taken on a different character this time. In the 1960s, it seemed safe to assume that the Soviets were ahead of us in teaching math and science, the two areas needed to build rocket ships. So we focused most of our reform efforts on those subjects. In the 1980s, however, it is not clear where we Americans are deficient. In comparing ourselves with the Japanese, it is a bit more difficult to pinpoint what classes are needed to build better cars.

Thus, our response is to compare the entire educational systems of the two countries. Or we compare American schools of the 1980s with American schools of some unspecified earlier period when American cars ruled the roads. The latter comparison seems more valid, since most of us are romantic enough to believe that the schools we attended were more demanding, more thorough, and more moral than the schools of today.

There is one other major difference between the school-reform movements of the sixties and the eighties. Following the *Sputnik* affair, Congress could not wait to get back into session to adopt the National Defense Education Act of 1958, which pumped millions of dollars into schools to buy teaching equipment, build laboratories, buy text materials, and retrain teachers. In contrast, in this decade, while everyone wants better schools, no one wants to pay for them. The 1983 report *A Nation at Risk*, the warning cry of the current crisis, suggested some far-reaching changes, but offered no advice whatsoever as to how these changes would be financed. Since 1983, many states have ordered changes for local schools, but again these mandates frequently arrive without funds.

Amid the differences, there is one similarity between the two eras of school reform. This similarity, common to almost all reform movements in history, is the conviction that there is only one way to improve our schools: Get tougher on kids. The proposals might sound grand when glibly preached by politicians, executives, and educators. These proposals include longer school days, longer school years, improved curriculum, fewer electives, early childhood opportunities, measurable standards of excellence, and more. But for the student, the bottom line is always the same: Life gets tougher.

Few people have ever talked about reforming schools in terms of making them more fun, or easier, or more relevant, or more practical. And we usually disregard such questions as, "How much pressure are our young people *already* under?" and, "How much more pressure can they endure?" Rather, we stick to our creed, not realizing that the most dangerous characteristic of school reform in the 1980s could well be the pressure it places on kids.

In assessing problems in education, it is not enough to look at the legislation, or the new mandates, or even the test scores. We must also consider what school reform looks like from the student's point of view. To ascertain what is actually happening in this era, we need to look at what is happening to average young people in this country on a day-to-day basis.

What has happened in their lives in the past five years, and what effect will that have on the kinds of people they will become in the next ten years? As reformers and revolutionaries have always known, a price must be paid for change. What is that price today? Who is paying for the recent changes in school programs? With these questions in mind, let us now examine some of the recent proposals for school reform:

Increase school hours. This mandate has been carried out in several ways. Some states have lengthened the school day. Some have increased the school year. Other states have defined attendance regulations in stricter language, specifying excused and unexcused absences and severely punishing students who accumulate unexcused absences.

At the root of such proposals is the notion that more is better. As the thinking goes, if students are not learning anything in a six-hour day, they should go to school for seven hours. If students aren't learning anything in 180 days, they should go to school for 200 days.

Yet there are two intriguing implications in this reasoning. The first involves a seeming inconsistency in the assessment of what students accomplish while in school. Going to school more presumes there is actually something valuable happening there. But this is a presumption with which many reformers seem to disagree. Indeed, if these critics believe much of what they say about the inadequacy of education, it would make better sense to shorten both the school day and year!

The second implication is the presumption that not much of value is happening at home. To explain: On the one hand, educators and politicians are crying for more parental involvement in decisions relating to their children's education. On the other hand, they ask for more hours for children at school, a request that suggests parents really don't know what to do with their children in the first place.

The proposal that children need more hours at school is one that should be seriously considered before being accepted. Disregard for a moment any mental pressure an extra hour a day might add to a student's load and consider just the physical ramifications. I doubt that comfort has ever been much of a factor in the designing and choosing of school furniture. In fact, most church pews are far more comfortable than school desks. Think about yourself sitting quietly for six hours in a church pew, with a big, stern person staring at you should you even think of wiggling. Now think about staying one more hour.

Adding an hour a day to a seven-year-old's confinement is a major demand. We need to be aware of that when considering ways to improve the quality of that student's learning.

Increase teaching efficiency. During most of the 1970s, teaching was defined largely in terms of a relationship between teacher and student. This concept was manifested in various ways, but the general goal of teachers was to build relationships. The educational gurus and literature that told us how to be more effective talked in terms of the all-important teacher-student relationship.

In the 1980s, not only has this model disappeared, but it has become an example of what teaching is supposedly *not* to be. This is the age of teaching "efficiency." And according to this contemporary model, if teachers are properly committed to their task, they simply will not have time to spend on relationships. The goal is to get through the lesson; all else is at best secondary.

The new model of education equips teachers with methods, with step-by-step strategies for lesson planning and implementation. There is no room for creativity or casual talk. In some schools, when a student misbehaves, his or her name is written on a blackboard. Taking class time to talk with the student about his or her conduct is inefficient; it slows down the lesson.

Efficiency is impersonal. One machine feeds students all the data they need to know; another machine scores their tests. Administrators instruct teachers to teach from bell to bell, lest a precious moment be lost. When one lesson is finished, the next is begun. Homework, of course, is required—the more the better.

Obviously, some programming and methodology is necessary. But when carried to the extreme—as it is in many classrooms under the banner of school reform—it can produce not only intense pressure for students, but, ironically, mediocrity—the very thing we are trying to eliminate.

Almost every day I wander into a junior-high or high-school classroom just to observe what is happening. Some days I sit in three or four different classes. On occasion, I try to keep score of pieces of new information I pick up in a class period. It is not unusual for me, a middle-aged Ph.D., to pick up as many as thirty or forty pieces of new information in any given class period. These are pieces of knowledge presumably valuable enough to have found their way into the teacher's arsenal and probably valuable enough to find a spot on a future test. In just one class period, students are held accountable for thirty to forty pieces of new information! Multiply that by the number of classes a student has per day and you get some idea of the burden created by "efficiency instruction."

Given such a heavy load, students essentially have two options. The first is to try to grasp all this information. They can forego television and socializing, including family activities, to study. They can cram and hurry and learn as much as they can in order to pass the test.

Or they can learn to take the cheap way out—not listening in class, reading only the topic sentences of assignments, doing inferior work, borrowing notes from friends, treating homework as a group project. In other words, they can learn to cheat.

As a frequent visitor in classrooms around the country, I am convinced that it is almost impossible for any student to do quality work on every assignment he or she receives. Average and even above-average students must learn to cut corners just to complete the projects. The current method of instruction—driven by the perceived crisis and need for school reform—is teaching our students to be mediocre scholars. It is teaching quantity, not quality; getting by, not getting an education.

What amazes me is that I see a great majority of students still trying to stay on top. Last spring, I visited a high school during finals week. Finals *week*. (When I was a student in the good old days, when we still wrote with a number-two pencil on a Big Chief tablet, we had a finals *day*, and many of us were exempted from that if we had some combination of good grades and good attendance. Now there is a finals week, from which no one is exempted.)

At the school I visited, students take a two-hour final in each class, with a ten-minute break in between. I happened into a bathroom during one of those breaks. The 14- and 15-year-old scholars were there, stretching and flexing and trying to relieve the obvious tension from their shoulders, arms, and minds. I was touched with a sense of *déjà vu*, and then I remembered where I had last seen that kind of scholastic pressure. It was in 1973, when I took the examinations for my doctoral degree. But the tense and tired faces around me now were not those of 35-year-old professionals on their way up. These were 14-year-old kids trying to pass Algebra 1.

Not long ago, I visited a world history class where a young intern was working under the supervision of a thirty-year veteran teacher. The intern had taught these sophomores some material and had given them time to prepare for a test. Some of the students did not understand one portion of the information, so they asked the veteran, who held a master's degree in world history, to explain it to them. He responded, "I'm sorry, but I don't know that material myself."

Later, while talking with the two teachers, I questioned the value of learning the material. They could not see my point. It was historically accurate material, they said, and it took some tough mental work to master it. In so many words they told me that this is what teaching history is all about. What bothered me most about their comments was the fact that probably 22 of those 25 sophomore students stayed up late the night before to learn historical data that even their own teacher apparently felt was not worth knowing. I came away from the experience admiring high-school students, and concerned about what we are doing to them in the name of educational excellence.

Increase core courses and drop electives. The move to increase requirements for high-school graduation is widespread. We have reasoned that every high-school graduate—regardless of his or her ability or goals—should have at least four years of English, three years of math, one year of computer, three years of history, three years of science, and a foreign language thrown in for good measure. Why these are better than courses in such areas as shop, or homemaking, or typing, or even music, is not always clear. But one thing is certain: They must be better because they are tougher.

The current curriculum is certainly good for some students. But the assumption that all students have the same abilities and goals, and therefore need the same classes, is woefully misguided. Some are created with a talent for words; others have a gift for working with their hands. When a course emphasizes only skill with words, what is communicated to those whose talents lie elsewhere? In effect we say, by our actions if not by our statements, "You are a second-class citizen because your God-given gift is worthless here."

In the past, unfortunately, schools have communicated just such a message all too often. And the push for tougher graduation requirements has made the situation even worse.

For one thing, we may be hamstringing ourselves with this unrestrained push for excellence. While we cry for instruction in computer science, nearly 25 percent of the students entering the college where I teach do not know how to type on a keyboard. In other words, they are not as far along as they could be because they did not have the time during high school to take a simple typing class. We are cheating these people.

Of greater concern, however, are those who have valuable manual skills with no opportunity to develop them during their formative years. Some reform measures not only would deny them a chance to develop their skills, but would also deny them a chance to develop as persons, persons who need accomplishments and dreams as much as the college-bound graduate. What value messages are these students receiving?

As a teacher in 1963, I made friends with a high-school senior who could not read. He was a tall, handsome fellow who worked after school for an electrical contractor in a small town. He and I visited frequently and enjoyed each other's company. One day, I inadvertently discovered his secret, and since I was the only teacher who knew it, he and I became close friends. We even worked together on his reading for some time, without much progress. For whatever reason, he just couldn't master the art. Because he worked harder than most, and because he took several shop classes, he graduated from high school.

Not long ago I had a chance to visit him. What I found might surprise you. He still lives in that small town, but now he owns his own electrical contracting business. He is an active community leader, a deacon in his church, and the father of three daughters who are attending college. He is a sharp chess player and delightful conversationalist, well versed on international as well as local affairs. But he still can't read beyond an elementary level.

The last thing I want to do by telling this story is dismiss illiteracy as a problem. The inability to read is a tragedy, resulting in major limitations in life. In the case of my friend, his wife does a lot of reading for him, thus helping him to be successful even though he reads poorly.

But my point is this: What does a tough, word-oriented, required curriculum (including, possibly, a foreign language requirement) do to a fellow like that? Does it prepare him for life and build his appreciation for what God has made in him? Or does it tell him he is second-class?

Intensify early childhood education. It all sounds rather scientific and progressive: educational preschools and academic kindergartens. It now takes intense preschools to prepare students for the pressures of all-day, highly academic kindergarten. And for those who "fail" kindergarten, there are pre-first grades to help them catch up.

Last fall, one of my young friends was reprimanded for not being able to write his name on the first day of kindergarten. In my town, at least, five-year-olds are now expected to know what six-year-olds used to be taught. Six-year-olds are expected to know what eight-year-olds used to be expected to know. Eight-year-olds are doing junior-high work, and junior-high students are preparing for the college curriculum they will get in high school.

If we keep moving at this frantic pace in the name of educational excellence, more and more children will become adults before their time. We will lose the model of the child that Christ held on his lap when he said, "Unless you become like this child, you won't inherit the kingdom."

Nearly everyone I meet agrees this is a serious problem. But nobody is willing to do anything about it. Those who write books about the dangers of hurrying children get richer, yet we continue to applaud programs to hurry children. When it appears we might finally become more sensible, another television special tells us that children in Japan start school at age three, and we start the rush all over again.

Raise test scores. We cannot objectively measure how much fun school is, or how much students incorporate such concepts as good citizenship and virtue. Yet there is a need to measure educational achievement in specific, definable terms. So we depend on testing to tell us how much material students have mastered. The process, though somewhat flawed, is necessary.

But this age of school reform is characterized by an obsession with testing. Test scores are used to prove everything from who should be promoted, to who should teach, to which school is the best.

In our state, a new mandate requires each school to publish a "school report card." It contains a variety of information, yet the one statistic that makes the best newspaper copy, and thus gets the most headlines, is the average American College Test (ACT) score of the seniors. I know of people who have based their decision on which home to buy on ACT scores of local high-school students.

Neither the test makers nor the test givers intended the examinations to be used this way. The commonly stated purpose of most testing programs is to determine the success of a specific educational program and what changes should be made. But test results have become a matter of civic pride. The whole enterprise of education has been reduced to what can be measured by these numbers. Teachers teach with the intention not of increasing knowledge, but of raising test scores. And students are caught up in these misguided efforts.

Time to unwind

Despite my criticisms of current trends, I like America's schools. I like them because I like living in America, and I am just naïve enough to believe that schools have something to do with the quality of life in the society they serve. I see the need for some improvement.

But I do not believe a major overhaul is necessary.

In addition to schools, I am excited about American students. As I travel to schools throughout the country, I am impressed with students individually and collectively. Certainly there are problem cases. But the vast majority of the students I see are cheerful, industrious young people who are working hard to develop themselves and their talents.

I see these students fighting their way through crowded halls to get to class on time; staying mentally alert for seven-hour days while they try to absorb hundreds of pieces of new information; eating lunch in five minutes; completing three or four hours of homework a night; and keeping their sanity through it all. In short, I find students wound about as tight as we can wind them.

They didn't invent permissiveness on television or movies; they didn't invent rock music or drug abuse; they didn't invent casual sex or unrestricted profanity. Yet some strange sense of moral paternalism causes us to be shocked when our children live in the culture we gave them.

In short, American schoolchildren did not invent the problems of American society, and I doubt seriously that the current school-reform movement—replete with the value messages it is sending—is going to solve those problems. In fact, I am cautious of the possible outcome, because I remember the sixties.

CREATING
SOLUTIONS

Chapter 8

MORAL LITERACY AND THE FORMATION OF CHARACTER

William J. Bennett

When the call for "cultural literacy" went out several years ago, William Bennett was among the first to champion its cause. "To be culturally literate is to possess the basic information needed to thrive in the modern world," wrote E. D. Hirsch in his best seller, Cultural Literacy: What Every American Needs to Know. *A working knowledge of people, places, and events, Hirsch argued, is essential if we are to communicate effectively with one another, let alone make our society work.*

In the following essay, former Secretary of Education Bennett champions another sort of literacy—moral literacy. Based on his observations from visits to more than 100 schools across the country, Bennett insists there is widespread agreement on the elements of good moral character, and a consensus that schools should indeed be nurturing personal morality in young people. But that task is impossible if students are not exposed to examples of character, or do not possess even the words and ideas needed to discuss moral issues.

With the same outspokenness that characterized his tenure in public office, Bennett takes aim at the "specter of awful complexity" often raised when discussion of values in public education begins. "We should demystify this subject," he writes, so we can get down to the business of building character. How? Through the simple power of a story.

This chapter is adapted from an address delivered to the Manhattan Institute, New York City, October 30, 1986.

Moral principles and individual character are central to the Christian faith. But they have important political consequences as well. Moral principles are an anchor of democracy. Alexis de Tocqueville, in his critique of American society, wrote that morality is "the best security of law and the surest pledge of the duration of freedom." The teaching of values in our schools, as both a way to nurture the character of the young and safeguard our republic, is essential for our educational enterprise.

The term *values* itself is one that I have never particularly liked. It suggests that judgments of right and wrong, noble and base, just and unjust, are mere personal preferences, that things are worthwhile only insofar as individuals happen to "value" them. As a friend once said, when he hears the word *values* he reaches for his Sears catalog. Rather than reach for a catalog, we need to reach for new terms. Because these issues are not matters of mere personal taste, I suggest we relabel the enterprise now known as the "teaching of values" as, instead, the effort to help in the "formation of character" and the "achievement of moral literacy" among the young. These, I think, are what our goals should be.

A mighty auxiliary
First, consider the formation of character Forming character must begin in the home, starting in the earliest childhood years, but after that, schools must help—because, as President Charles Eliot of Harvard once reminded us, "in the campaign for character no auxiliaries are to be refused." And the school, like the church, can be a mighty auxiliary.

I would uphold this role as a proper one for our schools, even given the diversity of our society, for there is a fairly general agreement as to what elements constitute good character in an individual. You won't find many people who are going to argue: "No, honesty is not a part of good character," or "No, courage isn't really admirable." We all agree on the importance of these things. Now, we may disagree on cases involving these traits, or when there are conflicts among competing claims, but we still maintain our allegiance to good character as a virtue, as something worth preferring.

Most Americans want their schools to help form the character of their children. Responding to a 1984 Gallup poll, the American people said they wanted two things above all others from their schools: first, that schools teach our children how to speak and write correctly; and second, that they help students develop reliable standards of right and wrong.

These views have deep roots in America. At the time of our nation's founding, Thomas Jefferson listed the requirements for a sound education in the Report of the Commissioners for the University of Virginia. In this landmark statement on American education, Jefferson wrote of the importance of calculation and writing, and of reading, history, and geography. But he also emphasized the need "to instruct the mass of our citizens in these, their rights, interests, and duties, as men and citizens." Jefferson believed education should aim at the improvement of both one's "morals" and "faculties."

But today, despite the beliefs of the majority of Americans, no sooner does anyone begin to point out how important it is to "teach values" in the schools than others immediately begin to raise the specter of awful complexity. As soon as someone starts talking about forming character at school, others claim that it just cannot be done, that we will not find a consensus on what to teach or how to teach it. I have heard this complaint on and off—mostly on—during the more than fifteen years I have been writing on this issue.

A well-known columnist, for example, has written that if the people urging schools to teach values—including, he wrote, New York Governor Mario Cuomo and myself—were asked to define those values, we would probably find it hard to agree. Another columnist, also writing about me and the governor, gave this analysis: "In the United States, the most heterogeneous nation in the world, one man's values can be another man's anathema. . . . Does it really make any sense to add still further to [our schools'] burden, to insist that they provide the answers to questions of values upon which we mature adults cannot agree?"

Sometimes it is one and the same person who calls attention to the importance of teaching values and then immediately thinks better of his suggestion. For instance, Governor Cuomo, talking about his plans to bolster the teaching of values in New York schools, immediately demurred: "[We] probably won't be able to get a consensus view on values, so it probably won't go anywhere, but we'll try."

Toward a reasonable consensus

Governor Cuomo is right to stress the importance of teaching values—but he should not be so doubtful that it can be done. I agree there are hard cases. Nevertheless, this task can be done, and should be done. It has been done for most of American history. While a certain amount of caution and prudence is healthy, of course—no one wants to impose a moral straitjacket on children—we do not want to present them with a moral vacuum, either. There is no reason for excessive timidity in suggesting a role for our schools in the formation of character. In fact, there is an increasingly broad consensus today as to the importance of this task. According to a 1987 article in the *Washington Post,*

> the need to teach values in public schools, a theme pushed by conservatives for the past several years, is being promoted by liberals and leading educators as well, creating an unusual consensus that the nation's schools should abandon the "values-neutral" teaching approach widely used for two decades. The consensus is that schools should impart civic virtue and take clear positions on right and wrong behavior and personal morality.

I believe that our schools have a role to play in the formation of a child's character, that it can be done, and that we should demystify this subject so we can get down to business.

Some people argue we cannot agree on "values." Well, we cannot agree on everything. But we can agree on the basic traits of character we want our children to have and that we want our schools to develop. And we can agree that there ought to be such a thing as moral literacy.

What do I mean by "moral literacy"? Professor E. D. Hirsch, author of *Cultural Literacy*, has pointed out that being literate, in the usual sense of the term, entails more than recognizing the forms and sounds of words. Being literate is also a matter of building up a body of knowledge enabling us to make sense of the facts, names, and allusions cited by an author. This background knowledge Hirsch calls "cultural literacy."

For example, someone who is unsure who Grant and Lee were may have a hard time understanding a paragraph about the Civil War, no matter how well he or she reads. Likewise, a reader who is not familiar with the Bill of Rights will not fully understand a sentence containing the words *First Amendment*. Understanding a subject, then, involves not just the possession of skills; it also depends on the amount of relevant, prior knowledge a reader has—his or her cultural literacy.

So it is with "moral literacy." If we want our children to possess the traits of character we most admire, we need to teach them what those traits are. They must be able to identify the forms and content of those traits. They must achieve at least a minimal level of moral literacy that will enable them to make sense of what they will see in life, and, we may hope, will help them live it well.

The business of teaching character

How can education form character and help students achieve moral literacy? It seems that some have forgotten the answer. Some educators have turned to a whole range of "values education" theories, wherein the goal is to guide children in developing "their own values" by discussion, dialogue, and simulation. It is not unusual to hear educators say they should be neutral toward questions of right and wrong. I believe these views are mistaken.

For example, in 1985 the *New York Times* ran an article quoting New York-area educators proclaiming that "they deliberately avoid trying to tell students what is ethically right and wrong." The article told of one counseling session involving fifteen high school juniors and seniors. In the course of that session the students concluded that a fellow student had been foolish to return $1,000 she found in a purse at the school. According to the article, when the students asked the counselor's opinion, "He told them he believed the girl had done the right thing, but that, of course, he would not try to force his values on them. 'If I come from the position of what is right and what is wrong,' he explained, 'then I'm not their counselor.' "

Now, once upon a time, a counselor offered counsel, and he or she knew that an adult does not form character in the young by taking a stance of neutrality toward questions of right and wrong or by merely offering "choices" or "options."

We would do well to remember that the Greek word *charaktēr* means "enduring marks," traits that can be formed in a person by an almost infinite number of influences. But as the theologian Martin Buber pointed out, the educator is distinguished from all other influences "by his will to take part in the stamping of character and by his consciousness that he represents in the eyes of the growing person a certain selection of what is, the selection of what is 'right,' of what should be." It is in this will, Buber says, in this clear standing for something, that the "vocation as an educator finds its fundamental expression."

To put students in the presence of a morally mature adult who speaks honestly and candidly to them is essential to their moral growth. Is this not why many teachers entered the profession in the first place—because they thought they could make a positive difference in the lives of students, in the development of their character, to make them better men and women?

We must have teachers and principals who not only state the difference between right and wrong, but who make an effort to live out that difference in front of students. In this business of teaching character, there has never been anything as important as the quiet power of moral example.

When I visited a class at Waterbury Elementary School in Waterbury, Vermont, I asked the students, "Is this a good school?"

"Yes," they answered.

"Why is this a good school?" I asked.

Among other things, one eight-year-old said, "The principal, Mr. Riegel, makes good rules and everyone obeys them."

"Give me an example," I said.

After a moment of thought, he answered, "You can't climb on the pipes in the bathroom. We don't climb on the pipes and the principal doesn't either."

This example is probably too simple to please a lot of people who want to make this topic difficult, but there is something profound in the answer of that child, something educators should pay more attention to. You cannot expect children to take messages about rules or morality seriously unless they see adults taking those rules seriously in their day-to-day affairs. Certain things must be said and certain examples must be set—there is no other way. These are the first and most powerful steps in nurturing character and developing moral literacy in the young.

The moral of the story

When it comes to instilling character and moral literacy in schoolchildren there is, of course, the question of curriculum. What materials and texts should students be asked to read? The research shows that most "values education" exercises and separate courses in "moral reasoning" tend not to affect children's behavior; if anything, they may leave children morally adrift. So what kind of materials should we be using instead?

The simple answer is that we do not have to reinvent the wheel. And we do not have to add new courses. We have a wealth of material to draw on—material that virtually all schools once taught to students for the sake of shaping character. We have easily at hand subject matter that we can teach in our regular courses, in our English and history classes. We can invite our students to discern the morals of stories, of historical events, of famous lives.

For example:

Do we want our children to know what honesty means? Then we might teach them about Abe Lincoln walking three miles to return six cents. Conversely, we might teach about Aesop's shepherd boy who cried wolf.

Do we want our children to know what courage means? Then we might teach them about Joan of Arc, Horatius at the bridge, Harriet Tubman and the Underground Railroad.

Do we want them to know about kindness and compassion, and their opposites? Then they should read *A Christmas Carol* and *Anne Frank: The Diary of a Young Girl*, and later on, *King Lear*.

Do we want them to know about loyalty to country? Then we should want them to know of Nathan Hale, about the Battle of Britain, and about the siege at Thermopylae. They should know that men such as Lt. Elmo Zumwalt have served their country willingly, nobly. And they should understand the contrary examples of men like Benedict Arnold and John Walker.

We want our children to know what faithfulness to family and friends means, and so they should know how Penelope and Telemachus and even an old dog waited 20 years for Odysseus to come home. We want them to know about respect for the law, so they should understand why Socrates told Crito: "No, I must submit to the decree of Athens."

We want them to know about persistence in the face of adversity, and so they should know about the Donner party, and the voyages of Columbus, and the character of Washington during the Revolution, and Lincoln during the Civil War. Our youngest should be told about *The Little Engine that Could.*

We want our children to recognize greed, and so they should know King Midas. We want them to recognize vanity, and so they should read Shelley's "Ozymandias," and they should learn about Achilles. We want them to know about overreaching ambition, so we should tell them about Lady Macbeth.

We want our children to know that hard work pays off, so we should teach them about the Wright brothers at Kitty Hawk and Booker T. Washington learning to read. We want them to see the dangers of an unreasoning conformity, so we should tell them about the emperor's new clothes and about Galileo. We want them to see that one individual's action can make all the difference, so we should tell them about Rosa Parks, and about Jonas Salk's discovery of a vaccine against polio.

We want our children to respect the rights of others, and so they should read the Declaration of Independence, the Bill of Rights, the Gettysburg Address, and Martin Luther King, Jr.'s "Letter from Birmingham City Jail."

There are other stories we can include, too—stories from the Bible: Ruth's loyalty to Naomi, Joseph's forgiveness of his brothers, Jonathan's friendship with David, the Good Samaritan's kindness toward a stranger, Cain's treatment of his brother Abel, David's cleverness and courage in facing Goliath. These are great stories, and we should be able to use them in teaching character to our children.

Why? Because they teach moral values we all share. And they should not be thrown out just because they are in the Bible. As

Harvard psychiatrist Robert Coles recently asked, "Are students really better off with the theories of psychologists than with the hard thoughts of Jeremiah and Jesus?" Knowing these hard thoughts is surely part of moral literacy, and discussing them does not violate our Constitution.

Laying hold of the task ahead

These, then, are some of the familiar accounts of virtue and vice with which our children should be familiar. Do our children know these stories? Unfortunately, many do not. They do not because in some places we are no longer teaching them. Why should we go to the trouble of picking up the task again? For several reasons.

First, these stories and others like them are interesting to children. Of course, the pedagogy will need to be varied according to students' level of comprehension, but you cannot beat these stories when it comes to engaging the attention of a child. Nothing in recent years, on television or anywhere else, has improved on a good story that begins "Once upon a time. . . ."

Second, these stories, unlike a course in "moral reasoning," give children some specific reference points. Our literature and history are a rich quarry of moral literacy. We should mine that quarry. Children must have at their disposal a stock of examples illustrating what we believe to be right and wrong, good and bad—examples illustrating that, in many instances, what is morally right and wrong can indeed be known.

Third, these stories help anchor our children in their culture, its history and traditions. They give children a mooring. This is necessary because morality, of course, is inextricably bound both to the individual conscience and the memory of society. Our traditions reveal the ideals by which we wish to live our lives. We should teach these accounts of character to our children so that we may welcome them to a common world, and in that common world to the continuing task of preserving the principles, the ideals, and the notions of greatness we hold dear.

I have not mentioned issues such as nuclear war, abortion, creationism, or euthanasia. This may come as a disappointment to some people, but the fact is that the formation of character in young people is educationally a different task from—and a prior task to—

the discussion of some of the difficult controversies of the day. But first things first. We should teach values the same way we teach other things: one step at a time. We should not use the fact that there are indeed many difficult and controversial moral questions as an argument against basic instruction in the subject. We do not argue against teaching biology or chemistry because gene splicing and cloning are complex and controversial, against teaching American history because there are heated disputes about the Founders' intent. Every field has its complexities and controversies. And every field has its basics.

So, too, with forming character and achieving moral literacy. You have to walk before you can run, and you ought to be able to run straight before you are asked to run an obstacle course. The moral basics should be taught in school, in the early years. The tough issues, if teachers and parents wish, can be taken up later. And, I would add, a morally literate person will be immeasurably better equipped than a morally illiterate one to reach a reasoned and ethically defensible position on these tough issues.

Further, the task of teaching moral literacy and forming character is not political in the narrow meaning of the term. People of good character are not all going to come down on the same side of difficult political and social issues. Good people—people of character and moral literacy—can be conservative, and good people can be liberal; good people can be religious, and good people can be nonreligious. But we must not permit our disputes over thorny political or religious questions to suffocate the obligation we have to offer instruction to our young people in the area in which we have, as a society, reached a consensus: namely, on the importance of good character, and on some of its pervasive particulars.

During my term as secretary of education, I spent a lot of time traveling the country, visiting schools and teaching classes. I taught seventh graders the Declaration of Independence, and eleventh graders *Federalist* No. 10 and the story of the Constitutional Convention. To third graders I taught the story of Cincinnatus returning to his farm when he could have had an empire. To the third graders, too, I've taught how nothing but George Washington's exemplary character stood against a mutinous army of unpaid soldiers bent on besieging the Continental Congress in Philadelphia, and how that shining character itself was enough to make those men turn back. And they understood.

I taught these lessons, and others, to American children. I tried to teach them directly and unapologetically. I talked to teachers and parents about these matters as well. And when I did this publicly in our classrooms, no one ever stood up and said, "You shouldn't be teaching these lessons. You are indoctrinating our children, corrupting them; you are not respecting parental prerogative. This isn't the right stuff for our children to learn." On the contrary, people were pleased. It has been my experience, in many trips across this country, that students and parents welcome such discussions; they want more, and most teachers and principals are not opposed to giving them more. There is a very broad, and very deep, consensus out there, and we are failing in our duty if we ignore it. Objections noted, cautions observed, let us get down to—and back to—the business of the moral education of the young.

Chapter 9

BEYOND THE LESSON PLAN: CURRICULUM AND VALUES

Rick Little

What makes a school a good school? Test scores? Discipline? School spirit? Teachers? Textbooks? Parents? The elements of the formula are not easy to identify or mix in the proper proportion. But when they are skillfully combined, they create one of the most important, and most misunderstood, elements in public education: curriculum.

Curriculum is much more than books, worksheets, and lesson plans, says Rick Little, chairman of Quest International, a nonprofit organization that works with schools to create and implement values-education programs. Often well-intentioned Christians focus their efforts only on textbooks or courses, usually in response to material they deem objectionable. But Little is also concerned about what some educators call "hidden curriculum"—the more subtle teaching and learning that includes what happens in the hallways and on the playground as well as within the classroom. This broad picture of curriculum, he says, communicates values to students as clearly as words written on a page.

During the past fifteen years in his work with Quest, Little has visited hundreds of schools and talked with thousands of administrators, teachers, students, and parents. More than a million young people currently participate in Quest's programs in thirteen thousand schools. In this chapter, Little offers specific suggestions to help parents and concerned community members find the right formula for their schools.

T he school auditorium was filled with angry, arguing parents. The community was divided against itself—"torn apart," as one mother said, "by a public-school system that is opposed to everything Christians believe and want taught to their children." No one was silent. Everyone seemed to have a strong opinion. The issue: teaching values in the public-school curriculum.

Scenes like this one are occurring across the nation as parents, community leaders, business people, and government officials grow increasingly concerned about the values, attitudes, and behaviors taught in public schools. Gallup polls repeatedly show that more than 80 percent of parents want public schools to teach moral values. The need is obvious. In the past two decades, teenage suicide has tripled, and teenage pregnancy has doubled. The United States now has the highest rate of adolescent pregnancy of all the world's industrialized nations, twice the rate of second-place Great Britain. American youth also have the highest levels of drug use of any young people in the industrialized world.

The list of problems could continue; and there is little debate on the need for solutions. The most pressing issue is where to find those solutions and then how to implement them.

Many point to the public-school curriculum as the source of problems—and the means of solutions. But what is curriculum? And how can it be used to promote such things as citizenship and moral values?

Focusing on the curriculum

Most parents or community leaders who want to make a difference in their local public schools turn almost instinctively to "the curriculum." Their aim is on target, for curriculum is indeed what the school is teaching. It is the best place to address the issue of values education. Often, however, parents and others do not understand exactly what curriculum is; their misunderstanding renders their efforts ineffective, and may even create more problems.

The word *curriculum* has come to have many meanings. The

majority of people think immediately of a curriculum guide or teacher's manual. To them a curriculum is a series of lesson plans, a course of study, educational goals and objectives, and student textbooks and worksheets. But the formal aspects of curriculum are not the only ones that communicate values. There is also a "hidden curriculum" that, whether structured or unstructured, shapes the values of students. Curriculum, according to this definition, is much more than what happens inside the four walls of a classroom; it is more than the chapters of a textbook. It is everything that happens in a school. It includes many different factors that teach kids specific messages and values just as clearly as if they were reading a textbook. These factors include:

The climate of the school. What is the feeling of the school? What are the attitudes of the adults in the school toward young people and toward each other? How do the students treat each other? Is it a school filled with tension, conflict, fighting, and put-downs?

These aspects of the school climate may not seem so important for values education at first, but a school with a negative climate can be teaching negative values without ever having students read or write about those values. Conversely, a school with a positive climate—where students and adults are concerned about one another and the world around them—can teach a profound sense of Christian caring and traditional ethics.

For example, in a school in central Ohio, students throughout the school spent most of a year writing letters to people in the community who were ill and bedridden. Some of these shut-ins even managed to visit classes at the school and meet their young pen pals. Everybody in the school got involved. What the children learned from writing to shut-ins carried over to the way everyone in the school treated one another. It doesn't take long in that building to discover it is a school in which people care about others.

Student discipline. Closely related to school climate, student discipline is always at the top of the list when parents and community members express their concerns about public schools today. How teachers discipline students is an important part of the curriculum—and a strong communicator of values. Effective school discipline combines high expectations of behavior with support, affirmation, and praise. We need to give kids enough rope so they can get burned, but not enough to hang themselves.

One school in the Midwest includes as part of its overall approach to discipline the idea of "catching kids being good." This school recognizes the importance of setting limits and enforcing consequences for misbehavior. But, in addition, everyone in the school, students included, is on the lookout for positive behavior. Every week examples of positive behavior are publicly recognized and applauded.

Parent involvement. Are parents kept well informed about what is happening at the school? Is there a regular newsletter, even just a typewritten sheet, sent home often? Do parents feel welcome in the school? All these aspects of parental involvement reflect another part of the curriculum. Schools that actively encourage parents' participation recognize parents as the primary educators of their children—and the primary source of values.

These are just a few examples of the kind of curriculum not found in a teacher's manual or textbook. Noted educational psychologist Benjamin Bloom says that perhaps more than 90 percent of the school day is composed of the "hidden curriculum"—that is, all of the noncognitive, nonacademic activities in which a child is involved.

As we think about ways to influence the values curriculum of our schools, therefore, we need to think as much about what is happening in the hallways and on the playgrounds—and between the school and home—as what is happening in the classroom.

What can parents and other interested Christians do to affect the curriculum—hidden and formal—in their schools? Obviously, if curriculum involves the whole environment of education, improving it means getting involved in many aspects of school life. What follows suggests ways that involvement can take place.

Learn about the school's structure

For parents and others to make a real impact on local schools, they need to understand how the two basic levels of the educational system—elementary and secondary—are different from each other.

Although the principal is a key figure at both levels, his or her support for anything a parent might propose will be especially crucial at the elementary level. Elementary-school faculties tend to be more unified, and often more child-centered, than faculties at the secondary level. Parents must keep in mind, though, that the pressure to "teach to the test"—that is, prepare students to do well on standardized tests of basic skills—is more intense at the elementary level.

At the secondary level, particularly in large junior and senior high schools, the departmental structure is more important. Often each department, guided by its chairperson, makes the key decisions about curriculum and textbooks.

The "hidden curriculum" can also be a more crucial consideration for secondary schools. Parents should take note of the kinds of clubs and extracurricular activities the school offers, and find out if the school is promoting healthy, positive involvements for kids. What is the school policy regarding smoking and drug use, and how consistently is it enforced? What about attendance and class cutting? Are they tolerated or neglected? Those are key indicators of how well the school is teaching students to respect the school, authority, and the very process of education itself.

Another important action relates to formal curriculum. Parents can determine if a school has a *curriculum advisory committee.* Many public schools are required to have parent advisory committees as part of special state or federal program funding. In many others, the principal or the superintendent of schools creates a standing committee of parent and community advisers. Parents can work to ensure that they are represented in the selection of specific materials and programs.

Finally, parents should not overlook the most obvious ways of getting involved in the schools. If the school has an active parent-teacher organization, for example, this can be an important means of getting to know the school and finding opportunities for influence and leadership. Parents can work to elect people to the board of education who reflect the values and beliefs they feel are important, choosing those people who will play a positive and constructive role.

Learn about the school's curriculum and programs
Although the "hidden curriculum" is just as important as what is

found in teacher's guides and textbooks, parents must not overlook the school's *written* curriculum. They need to get acquainted with the types of teaching and learning materials used in the school. Too often concerned parents and community members focus their attention on a single textbook or film without developing a real understanding of the other parts of the curriculum. Just as important in helping the school develop a clear, consistent approach to values education is knowing some of the basics of what the school is teaching.

One group of Christian parents I met with recently told me how they took the time to become acquainted with their school's drug-education program. They were concerned about the program's content, which focused on the factual information about drugs while neglecting the moral decision of whether or not to use drugs. "That's not what we want our children to be learning," one of the parents said. "We want the school to teach them that using drugs is *wrong*, and they shouldn't do it." By getting to know exactly what the program was and was not teaching about drug use, these parents were able to make a well-informed, reasonable presentation to the principal and influence a change in the drug-education program to include a clearer no use message.

Getting to know the written curriculum does not mean parents have to spend every night poring over textbooks. It can involve simply asking their children what they are learning in a particular subject. For people without children in the public schools, it can mean talking with young people at church or the children of friends and acquaintances.

Learn about educational issues in general
Parents need to get to know the educational system so well that teachers and administrators recognize the parents understand what they are experiencing—the constraints of the classroom, the scarcity of resources, the bureaucracy, and many other aspects of public education that parents also find frustrating.

That includes, among other things, taking time to understand the realities of teaching. Any parent knows the difficulty of meeting the needs of just two or three children. But imagine thirty-five twelve-year-olds at one time. Advocates for change need to remember that, on the average, nearly half those kids come to school each morning from homes where they do not live with both their natural parents. Six kids in every class are children of alcoholic parents. Nine are living in poverty and probably came to school without breakfast. Several may speak only limited English.

Parents should read about education and schools. They need to consider many different points of view. A journal such as *Phi Delta Kappan*, found at many libraries, tracks key educational trends.

If parents and concerned citizens can establish that they are knowledgeable about how the educational system works—that they can see it from the inside, so to speak—they will be way ahead of the game in trying to make an impact on that system. Otherwise, they will risk being perceived as outsiders who do not really understand what is going on in the schools, and who, therefore, cannot be relied on as a source of relevant ideas.

Encourage schools to develop new approaches to promoting values
Educators are often under so much pressure from all sides that the question of values education gets lost in the shuffle. "I wish we had more time to teach real-life skills," one elementary teacher told me when I visited her school. "Sometimes I think the most important value we're teaching kids today is that if they don't do well on those standardized tests, they're worthless. It's as if we're saying what they're like as people or what they believe in doesn't make a bit of difference."

As advocates of values education, the feedback of parents and concerned Christians can be an important factor in making values education part of the school's formal agenda. School administrators need to be encouraged to articulate a *schoolwide values-education plan*, developed with input from parents, staff, students, and community leaders. The plan should specify the values the school will teach and the ways it will teach them. It should represent a consensus about a core of values to be taught in a carefully considered, sequential approach—not just a list of "Thou Shalt Nots."

Developing such a plan is not an idealistic pipe dream; many school districts have already done it. In the Saint Louis, Missouri, area, for example, a consortium of school districts combined their resources to develop a communitywide survey of parents, educators, ministers, and other community representatives on what values education in the public schools should be. They then held a series of community forums, developed clear guidelines for values education, and set up task forces to implement the plan in their local schools. This kind of ambitious project can only be successful when the school, the community, and parents work together.

A values plan is much more than a list of rules; it needs to say which values are to be promoted (for example, honesty, truthfulness, and concern for others). It should also make the "hidden curriculum" an explicit element by calling for such aspects of positive values education as these:

Increased parental involvement in many different aspects of the life of the school, such as membership on existing committees, regular meetings of parents and teachers, and frequent communication between the school and home.

A *school climate committee*, with active participation of faculty members, support staff members, parents, students, and community members; this group can help to develop and implement schoolwide events that will create a strong sense of community and positive values in the school.

Service opportunities, like the letter-writing campaign of students in Ohio to shut-ins. Through their active involvement in providing service to others, kids learn important lessons about the values of caring and concern for others, postponing immediate gratification, taking responsibility, and setting and achieving goals. Increasingly, educators are recognizing service projects as an important element of students' learning at all grade levels.

The plan should also include strategies for creating a schoolwide "moral community." One aspect of this is conduct codes that translate moral values into widely understood and consistently enforced guidelines for behavior. Equally important is the need to give students an active role in upholding the school's moral standards, through, for example, a student government that gives students meaningful responsibilities. Studies of learning have repeatedly shown that young people truly internalize what they learn when they are active participants in learning. This is especially true of values education. It is appropriate for adults to set the rules and limits, but when we give young people an opportunity to participate in deciding *how* to enforce those limits and what the consequences will be for violating them, that is when the most valuable learning takes place.

Be an advocate, not an adversary

The best advice is simple and time tested. When it comes to influencing the curriculum of our public schools and instilling values in the midst of a moral vacuum, we need to proceed carefully and thoughtfully. We need to "know the territory" and convince educators that our goal is to help them do their main job—educating kids—even better.

Clearly, all schools are not created equal, and I have seen some classroom and school activities to which I am strongly opposed. These include the kind of teaching that involves little more than lecturing to kids, which defies both common sense and research about how kids learn. I likewise oppose programs that send mixed and confusing messages about issues such as drug abuse, issues that require clear expectations of behavior. The question is how do we, as Christians, make our concerns known and influence the content and character of our public schools? I believe our greatest hope lies in becoming advocates for what is right. Truth—as we should know— will always prevail.

This chapter began with the story of a meeting of angry parents in a school auditorium. What was the outcome of that meeting?

It could have ended in angry confrontation, leading to further problems and conflicts—and a predictable wall of resistance on the part of the administrators and teachers. Or it could have ended with a group of concerned parents and community members becoming well-informed about their public schools and growing into a positive force for lasting change and Christian values.

I have seen both outcomes. In every case, the deciding factor was not the size of the school, or its location, or its financial status. What made the difference was whether parents and teachers were willing to understand one another and work together to overcome the obstacles that separate them from one another and from their common goal—making a better life for the children in their care.

Chapter 10

WHAT IS LEGAL? WHAT IS NOT? RELIGION IN PUBLIC SCHOOLS

Samuel E. Ericsson

Since the early 1960s, when the Supreme Court struck down certain state laws requiring teacher-led opening prayers in public schools, there has been much confusion as to what kinds of religious activity in public schools are permitted by the Constitution. Such confusion has also affected the discussion of values in public education because of the close relationship of values to religious beliefs.

The reigning perception is that Christianity and Christian values have been shut out of the public classroom by the courts. But Sam Ericsson, executive director of the Christian Legal Society, sees several opportunities for Christian involvement in public education. As he shows in the following chapter, Christianity can indeed be studied in public schools when approached in an objective and academic, rather than devotional and promotional, manner. In addition, he says, recent laws give Christian students access to school facilities for religious meetings such as Bible studies.

A third, often overlooked opportunity for Christian values to be taught virtually alongside public-school curriculum is found in released-time programs. This well-established approach to religious instruction, Ericsson says, is thoroughly constitutional but has been abandoned by most states and is ignored by most evangelical churches.

Have the courts forced God out the schoolhouse door? Ten years ago, the answer was unclear. A patchwork of court decisions had left school officials and Christians alike confused over the relationship between public education and religion. Today, thanks to high-court decisions and legislative action, the picture is more sharply defined. And what emerges are opportunities for religious influence in public schools far broader than once imagined. This chapter will focus on three such opportunities.

The first section centers on what is constitutionally permissible concerning the teaching of religion in the public-school curriculum. The second section addresses the rights of high-school students to meet voluntarily on the campus for Bible studies under the federal Equal Access Act. The third section deals with the overlooked open door of religious "released time" education whereby students are released from the public schools during the school day for religious training.

Teaching religion in the public schools

While some Americans remain committed to the view that religion as such should not be taught in public schools, a large and growing number of parents, educators, and leaders alike now voice their opinion concerning the importance of teaching *about* religion in public education. (This would include the consideration of the beliefs and practices of religions; the role of religion in history and contemporary society; and religious themes in music, art, and literature.) But what is the appropriate place of religion in the public-school curriculum? How does one approach such issues as textbook content and values education?

The following questions and answers are designed to assist school boards, teachers, and parents as they make decisions about curriculum, and to assist educators as they teach about religion and religious values in ways that are constitutionally permissible, educationally sound, and sensitive to the beliefs of students and parents. These answers were originally published in a brochure entitled

"Religion in the Public School Curriculum." Proposed by the Christian Legal Society, the brochure was eventually endorsed by diverse religious and educational organizations, including the American Association of School Administrators, the American Federation of Teachers, the Baptist Joint Committee on Public Affairs, the National Association of Evangelicals, the National Council of Churches, the National Education Association, and the National School Board Association.

Is it constitutional to teach about religion in public schools?
Yes. In school-prayer cases of the 1960s (which ruled against state-sponsored school prayer and Bible reading), the U.S. Supreme Court indicated that public-school education may include teaching about religion. In *Abingdon* v. *Schempp,* Associate Justice Tom Clark wrote this opinion for the Court:

> It might well be said that one's education is not complete without a study of comparative religion or the history of religion and its relationship to the advancement of civilization. It certainly may be said that the Bible is worthy of study for its literary and historic qualities. Nothing we have said here indicates that such study of the Bible or of religion, when presented objectively as part of a secular program of education, may not be effected with the First Amendment.

What is meant by "teaching about religion" in the public school?
The following statements distinguish between teaching about religion in public schools and religious indoctrination: The school's approach to religion is *academic,* not *devotional.* The school may strive for student *awareness* of religions, but should not press for student *acceptance* of any one religion. The school may sponsor *study* about religion, but may not sponsor the *practice* of religion. The school may *expose* students to a diversity of religious views, but may not *impose* any particular view. The school may *educate* about all religions, but may not *promote* or *denigrate* any religion. The school may *inform* the student about various beliefs, but should not seek to *conform* him or her to any particular belief.[1]

Why should study about religion be included in the public-school curriculum?

Because religion plays a significant role in history and society, study about religion is essential to understanding both the nation and the world. Omission of facts about religion can give students the false impression that the religious life of humankind is insignificant or unimportant. Failure to understand even the basic symbols, practices, and concepts of the various religions makes much of history, literature, art, and contemporary life unintelligible.

Study about religion is also important if students are to value religious liberty, the first freedom guaranteed in the Bill of Rights. Moreover, knowledge of the roles of religion in the past and present promotes cross-cultural understanding essential to democracy and world peace.

Where does study about religion belong in the curriculum?

Wherever it naturally arises. On the secondary level, the social studies, literature, and the arts offer many opportunities for the inclusion of information about religions, such as their ideas and themes. On the elementary level, natural opportunities arise in discussions of the family and community life and in instruction about festivals and different cultures. Many educators believe that integrating study about religion into existing courses is an educationally sound way to acquaint students with the role of religion in history and society.

Special courses or units about religion may also be taught. Some secondary schools, for example, offer such courses as world religions, the Bible as literature, and the religious literature of the West and of the East.

Do current textbooks teach about religion?

Rarely. Recent textbook studies conclude that the most widely used textbooks largely ignore the role of religion in history and society. For example, readers of high-school U.S. history texts learn little or nothing about the great colonial revivals, the struggles of minority faiths, the religious motivations of immigrants, the contributions of religious groups to many social movements, major episodes of religious intolerance, and many other significant events of history. Education without appropriate attention to major religious influences and themes is incomplete education.

How does teaching about religion relate to the teaching of values?
Teaching about religion is not the same as teaching values. The former is objective, academic study; the latter involves the teaching of particular ethical viewpoints or standards of behavior.

There are basic moral values that are recognized by the population at large, such as honesty, integrity, justice, compassion. These values can be taught in classes through discussion, by example, and by carrying out school policies. However, teachers may not invoke religious authority in encouraging or enforcing these values.

Public schools may teach about the various religious and nonreligious perspectives concerning the many complex moral issues confronting society, but such perspectives must be presented without adopting, sponsoring, or denigrating one view against another.

Religious practice in public schools
There has been much controversy in recent years regarding the constitutionality of religious meetings by high-school students before and after school or during activity periods. But the rights of students to meet voluntarily on campus for Bible study, Christian fellowship, and other religious purposes was clarified and guaranteed on August 11, 1984, when President Ronald Reagan signed into law the Equal Access Act. The following questions and answers are designed to help high-school students, parents, teachers, and school administrators take advantage of this important law on their campus.

What is equal access?
The Equal Access Act makes it unlawful for schools to discriminate against student groups solely because their meetings will include speech of a religious, political, or philosophical nature. It does not require all high schools to allow such groups to meet under all circumstances. But if a school allows any noncurriculum-related student groups to meet on school property during noninstructional time, it cannot deny religious groups an equal opportunity to meet or equal access to school facilities. Such groups must be provided with a classroom or other appropriate space to conduct meetings.

To be sure that a group, such as a Bible study, is protected by the provisions of the act, it should follow these guidelines:

1. The group must be student initiated and student led, and membership in the group must be voluntary.

2. The group should not be sponsored by a teacher or any other school employee. Any school employee present at meetings should be there as a monitor only and should not participate in the content of the meetings.

3. The group's meetings should not be conducted or controlled by people from outside the school, such as pastors, parents, or representatives of other outside organizations. Such individuals should not attend meetings on a regular basis, but occasional outside speakers are permitted if other groups have this privilege.

4. The group's meetings should not interfere with the orderly conduct of regular school activities.

The key to determining whether or not a school must allow a Bible-study group to meet is to look at other groups that are allowed to meet. If any noncurriculum-related groups are allowed to meet, the school must allow religious groups to meet. The law does not define what "noncurriculum-related" means, and the courts are now addressing this issue. But any club not directly related to an academic subject taught by the school is probably noncurriculum-related. Examples of such groups include a chess club, archery club, drama club, cheerleaders, pom-poms, 4-H Club, and many other extracurricular groups.

What is not provided for under the Equal Access Act?

The Equal Access Act guarantees equal treatment, not special treatment. It does not give religious groups preference over other groups. They must follow the same procedures and rules as all other groups. If there is a waiting list for available rooms, they must take their place on the list. They must follow the school's standard rules regarding attendance, parental permission, and outside speakers.

How can a campus club be started?

The first thing that students wishing to start a new Bible-study group at their school should do is find out what the school's policy and procedures are for organizing new student groups. If the policy is in writing, they should ask for a copy. If it is unwritten, they should find out who makes the decision on approving new groups and ask that person to spell out exactly what information is required in order to make a decision. Once they have the policy they must follow it closely.

To be protected by the Equal Access Act a group must be *student initiated*. Therefore, the proposal made to school authorities should be the work of students. Teachers should be involved only in an advisory capacity. The proposal should clearly state the purpose of the group and provide all other information needed by the school.

Here is a sample of a proposal for a student Bible-study group. Note that this is only a sample and should be used only as a guide in drafting any specific proposal. Students should feel free to include any kind of appropriate activity they are interested in pursuing as a group.

PROPOSAL FOR A NEW STUDENT ORGANIZATION
NAME:
PURPOSE: The organization will be a nondenominational Bible-study group. Its purpose will be to promote the social, emotional, intellectual, and spiritual growth of members and help members resolve problems they face by the application of the teachings of their faith.
MEMBERSHIP: The organization will be open to all students on a voluntary basis.
LEADERSHIP: The leadership of the group will be composed of students elected by all of the members. No teachers will lead or otherwise participate in the group's meetings.
ACTIVITIES: Possible activities will include Bible reading, prayer, and discussion of related topics and the application of these to the everyday lives of members.
MEETINGS: Meetings will be held (before school/after school/during activity period) in a classroom or other room assigned by the school. Attendance will be taken by a faculty monitor or by members signing a roster.

What if problems occur?
If a school fails to observe the guarantees of the Equal Access Act, there are several practical steps students should take.

First, they should ensure that any problem is approached with a prayerful and Christlike attitude. To "win our rights" by bringing reproach on our Lord is a loss. Christians are instructed to give thanks in everything—even adversity—and to pray for those in authority, even if they oppose us. That includes even a hostile school administrator. Students should pray for the Lord to give all involved wisdom and a humble, teachable spirit.

Second, they need to find out what the school's policy is in regard to social, political, and other school groups, and then determine whether the school follows this policy consistently regarding the establishment of new groups or administers the policy on a "hit or miss" basis.

Third, students should speak directly with the school official specifically responsible for the decision. Again, students need to examine their attitude and motives. They must never assume that those in authority are operating out of bad motives or out of hostility toward religion or the students' beliefs in particular. Perhaps they do not know all of the facts or do not understand or even know of the law. Equal Access Act guidelines for school officials, attorneys, and others involved in implementing the act are available from sources such as the Christian Legal Society. Students should ask the school officials if they have a copy of the law or guidelines, and if they do not, help them to obtain a copy.

Finally, if the school administration does not allow a group to meet on campus, students should respectfully request a clear, written explanation of the decision. They may then wish to seek further advice from parents, Christian lawyers, or groups such as the Christian Legal Society.

Religious released-time education
During the past thirty to forty years, the Judeo-Christian world view that once characterized the American public-school system has been replaced in large part by one that is markedly secular. In response to this shift, many parents have chosen other ways to educate their children. The most common option has been church schools. In recent years, home schooling has also gained in popularity among Christian parents.

There is, however, another option open to those parents who

continue to send their children to public schools, for whatever reason, yet wish to counteract the secularism so prevalent in public education. Religious released-time education offers an established, effective opportunity to provide religious instruction—and religious values—to balance any secular content during the course of a school day. Briefly described, this program allows students to be released during the school day for religious instruction off campus.

What are some of the arguments favoring the adoption of a released-time program by a school district?

The following reasons have been used in support of adopting programs:

1. A released-time program, if properly established and administered, is constitutional. In holding certain such programs constitutional, the Supreme Court has said that a released-time program in which students were allowed to leave the school grounds for religious instruction was the same, in principle, as allowing individual students to miss school with their parents' permission in order to attend a family baptism or observe religious holidays.[2]

2. A released-time program respects the religious nature of the American people and accommodates the public schools to those needs. It is an opportunity for students to receive religious instruction that is otherwise forbidden in the public classroom under Supreme Court decisions.

3. A released-time program provides a means by which students can be exposed to teaching that builds and strengthens Christian values. This is especially important when peer pressure and the mass media bombard Christians with undesirable influences.

4. A released-time program can be designed to provide instruction in Christian literature, history, and themes that are necessary in order to appreciate more fully important works of art, music, and literature, and therefore necessary to a complete education. Although such instruction can be given in public schools if taught objectively without any attempt to influence the beliefs of the students, a released-time program relieves the school of the expense of the course and of being in the controversial and difficult position of supervising the content and instruction of such a course.

5. A released-time program recognizes and reinforces the consti-

tutionally protected right of parents to direct the religious upbring-ing of their children.

Can parents or religious groups legally require a school board to adopt a released-time program?

Generally, no. Although a released-time program may be constitu-tional, it is not a constitutional right of parents, religious groups, or students to have such programs.[3] Thus a state or school district cannot be compelled legally to adopt a policy allowing students to be excused for off-campus religious instruction during school hours.

The courts are generally reluctant to interfere in the daily opera-tion of a school and usually defer to the discretion of school boards in establishing educational policies. As a practical matter, this means that parents and churches must cooperate with school authorities in establishing and operating a released-time program. The first step should be to establish clearly the authority of the school district in allowing students to attend off-campus religious activities during school hours. Parents and religious groups should meet with school officials to explain the legality of such programs, pointing to exist-ing state law authorizing school boards to excuse students for released-time programs. They should also educate the officials as to the desirability of such a program.

Who may operate a released-time program?

Each community will have its own unique ethnic, cultural, and religious character to consider in establishing a program. An effec-tive program should seek to accommodate the religious needs of the students in the community.

Parents working with local churches and other religious groups in the community must initiate the programs. The local school district cannot take the initiative. It is common for various religious groups and denominations to form a common council. The council provides both the structure and the administration for the program. Each group or denomination retains control over the location, materials, and religious content of its own program.

What are the basic guidelines for financing and administering released-time programs?

The public schools can neither finance religious released-time programs nor become excessively involved in administering religious activities. The religious groups or the parents must bear the entire cost of the program.

Are there limits on the amount of time from which students may be released for religious instruction?
To some extent, yes. Before a program administrator begins discussions with public-school authorities about when and for how long the school will release program participants, the administrator should consult the applicable statutes and regulations to determine what limitations may exist. Usually the time permitted for religious released time ranges from one to three hours per week. The release of students for one hour per day has been allowed.

In order to avoid any significant disruption of the school's schedule and to minimize administrative involvement, the local school usually designates the period of the day during which the participating groups may receive students for religious activities. As a practical matter, if more than one religious group sponsors a released-time program, then all groups must meet at the same time. In at least one program, the students themselves designated which class period they wanted to use for religious instruction.

Which students may participate in a released-time program?
School districts can institute religious released-time programs for any grade level. All released-time programs have required students to have parental permission to participate.

How should parental consent be obtained?
Program administrators should choose the method for obtaining parental consent that will require the least amount of school involvement. The religious groups that sponsor the program should take primary responsibility for distributing consent forms to parents. In one case where a group wished to open its program to persons not members of its denomination, it obtained a student enrollment list from the public school and then mailed the consent cards to parents. If the group does not wish to offer the program to all students, it can distribute cards to a select group.

Where may released-time classes be conducted?

The Supreme Court has ruled that released-time classes may not be held on public-school grounds.[4] As long as classes are not conducted on public-school property, though, released-time instruction may be provided in any otherwise lawful location. Courts have allowed programs to be held in churches; in trailers located near, but not on, school grounds; in a seminary that was architecturally similar to the school and located on a lot adjacent to the school; and at religious centers off school grounds.

In what manner should students be released from their public-school classes to attend released-time classes?

School officials should excuse students for religious instruction in the same manner that they release students for other purposes. They should attempt to excuse students for released time in a manner that does not stigmatize either the students excused or those remaining. Public-school teachers and administrators should not comment on the released-time program or on the students who choose to attend or not to attend.

How should students be transported from public-school premises to released-time classes?

The Supreme Court has explained that the constitutional principle of accommodating the religious needs of the students by cooperating in released-time programs does not justify significant financial expenditures to assist those programs. Generally, religious organizations and parents must assume full responsibility for a student's attendance at religious activities.

May a school district or state count the time that students spend in a released-time program in its formula for allocating state funds ("funding credit")?

Yes. A school district may count released-time hours toward funding credit if the state allows it to do so.

How much supervision may the public schools exercise over the content and teaching of a religious released-time course?

Very little. Supervision of the content and teaching of a released-time course is generally not allowed, since it might excessively entangle the state in religious matters. On the other hand, if a school decides to give academic credit for religious instruction in a released-time course, it may inquire into the training of teachers and whether a particular course covers a subject for which "credit" could be given. But when a released-time program, even one that grants academic credit, is structured in such a way as to require state officials to monitor and judge what is religious and what is not religious in a private religious institution, then the entanglement inherent in such a determination may exceed permissible accommodation and offend the Establishment Clause of the First Amendment.

Unfortunately, many Christians have abandoned public education. They believe the reports that the Supreme Court has expelled God from the schools. But there are many opportunities available to Christians to integrate their faith on public-school campuses in a way that is consistent with the law. Teachers, students, and parents should faithfully use the open doors available to them to be salt and light in every corner of a fallen world, including public education.

Chapter 11

PARENTS AS PARTNERS WITH PUBLIC EDUCATION

Cliff Schimmels

In the opening chapter of this book, Ernest Boyer of the Carnegie Foundation for the Advancement of Teaching stated that, in the end, parents matter most in a child's moral development and education. In the final chapter of this anthology, Cliff Schimmels, professor of education at Wheaton College, turns his attention to parents and speaks directly to them—and to any concerned Christian who wishes to have a positive impact on public education.

As a parent, teacher, and coach, and most recently as a teacher of teachers, Schimmels has been involved with public education for thirty years. His experience has convinced him that the only way to educate young people effectively and completely is for parents and schools to join in active partnership. And he is convinced that one person—one parent—can make a difference, not only in the education of his or her own child, but in the academic and moral health of an entire school system.

Unfortunately, the relationship between parent and school today is most often characterized by distance and mistrust. Forming such a partnership will take work, Schimmels says. It places responsibilities on both parties. In the following chapter, Schimmels, the author of Parents' Most-Asked Questions about Kids and Schools, *offers practical tips on how to work with public schools as responsible partners in the education of our next generation.*

Parents in one state were worried about the safety of their children when they walked to school. According to state law, schools transported any student who lived more than one and one-half miles from the school building. However, those students who lived within that mile-and-a-half limit had to find their own means of getting to school. In Catoosa, that meant many students on their way to school had to walk along a major highway each morning, while buses passed them by. Parents started a letter-writing campaign to their state congressmen, and the law was amended to permit students who would otherwise travel a hazardous route to ride the bus.

Mel and Norma Gabler became concerned about the content of a textbook their children were using in their school in Texas. After some investigation, they discovered that the objectionable text was selected from a list approved by a state textbook committee. The Gablers went to an open meeting of that committee, and after some hearings and negotiations, the offensive texts were removed from the state-approved list.

Parents of students at Thompson Junior High School and Haines Junior High School in St. Charles, Illinois, became concerned about the threat of drug and alcohol abuse in their community. They first formed a committee, then went to the school officials for counsel and help. Together, parents and educators began an effective drug and alcohol education program, which includes concerts, retreats, dramas, clubs, and activities. Parents help cover the cost of many events and serve as helpers.

A school district in south Texas was plagued with two common problems: too many students and not enough money. With direction from local principals, citizens formed a volunteer organization that provides more than forty nonpaid workers who serve as lunchroom and recess supervisors, library assistants, and classroom aides. Since the program was instituted, student test scores have improved steadily.

These stories—all true—combine to make one point: Parents who do not like what is happening in the public schools in their communities can do something about it. They can find out how the system works and change things.

As simple as it sounds, that piece of advice is based not on naïve optimism, but on political realism. Public schools are, by design and historical precedent, local institutions. Although the federal government's role in education has increased in recent years, the primary responsibility for education remains with the individual communities.

Unfortunately, however, I talk to people every day who feel disenfranchised by the public-school system. They feel it is aloof or corrupt, and as such is completely out of touch with what parents and communities want for their children. For whatever reason, they feel alienated from one of the most significant projects of their lives: educating their own children.

Every day, however, I also see positive changes in schools that have been initiated, promoted, and implemented by parents who are armed with nothing more than concern about their schools and a willingness to work to make them better.

As I observe and listen to these two groups—the alienated and the active—I react with both confidence and caution. First, I am confident that individual citizens can make a difference. We need to approach schools with that confidence so as to make the most of recent trends in education that offer us an increased role in making decisions about education and supervising the education of our children.

My confidence is tempered, though, by the knowledge that such involvement comes with a price of responsibility. If parents are going to have a voice in what is happening to their children, they must develop some working expertise in education. It would be sad, indeed—both for our children and for the nation—to give the freedom of educational choice and the responsibility of decision making to people who are not prepared to handle that.

I know that parents cannot become authorities on education by reading the few pages that follow. But I do want to offer seven tips for working with schools that I have gathered through my years as a teacher, school administrator, frequent visitor to schools, parent, and interested citizen. I have seen what works and what does not work from both sides of the schoolhouse door. Above all, I have seen that anyone concerned with public education *can* make a difference with a little thought, preparation, and understanding.

Get firsthand information

Frequently someone starts criticizing schools by saying something like, "Let me tell you what happened to my neighbor's sister's niece," or, "Let me tell you what I read in the newspaper last week."

Most of the time we do not accept hearsay evidence. For example, we would never lend money to someone only on what we have heard about his character. We do not select a surgeon based on hearsay. Nor do we choose a church to attend on the basis of hearsay. But how much of what we believe about schools have we pieced together from second- or third- or fourthhand information?

The issue of education is simply too vital for us to accept and act upon hearsay information. With the present emphasis in our churches on the role of family, and the present cries of school reformers for more parental involvement in the education process, every citizen—and every parent in particular—must have an accurate idea of what is actually going on in schools, based on firsthand information.

There are several methods by which to gain this information. School people themselves, at least the good ones, know the value of having a knowledgeable constituency, so they provide several opportunities for people to come to school for a firsthand look. Parents, grandparents, aunts and uncles, and taxpayers in general should take advantage of each of these opportunities. Any person who does not attend the annual open house at the local school has lost credibility when criticizing that school in the same way that a person who does not vote has lost a platform on which to complain about the government.

If education is such an important issue in this country, why do schools see such meager attendance at such events as back-to-school nights—or even at parent-teacher conferences? Perhaps the real educational scandal is not what is happening in the classrooms but what is *not* happening at PTA meetings.

For a real look, parents should go to their children's school during the school day. They can easily think of some reason to go. For example, they can plan to pick up their child at the end of the day but arrive a little early and look around. Or they can deliver a child's lunch during the morning. Parents should use any excuse to walk through the halls so they can get an idea of what is happening.

Concerned parents can call the principal and ask to visit. Most principals feel about their schools like grandparents feel about their grandchildren: They welcome any opportunity to show them off. Visitors should be prepared to stay longer than they might expect.

If cursory visits such as these do not yield an accurate view, interested parties should volunteer for some regular duty at a school. A pastor I know was confused by all the conflicting reports he heard concerning the quality of public education, so he phoned a local high-school principal simply to gather more information. Today he spends two hours a week as a teacher's aide in a special-education class. Not only has that pastor become a highly respected source of information about the school, he is also directly contributing to the lives of many of its students.

School-board meetings are always open to the public (except on occasions when individual personnel matters are discussed) and are a good source of firsthand information. Any local school district office has information about the time and place of its board meetings.

Implementing these suggestions may sound like a lot of hard work. It is. Educating children is not an easy business. But on the other hand, attending a school-board meeting takes no more time than watching a television special that proposes to tell the "real story" of American education.

Know who makes the decisions

Grumbling to the salesclerk at the cash register about shoddy merchandise probably will not improve quality control at the factory. Likewise, yelling at an office receptionist about a confusing school policy may start an argument, but very likely it will not change the policy. To effect change, one must go to the source of a decision, or to whomever has the authority to deal with a situation. In most schools, decisions come from several sources.

For example, a classroom teacher seems to have an attendance policy that seems a little unfair. Perhaps the teacher set the policy.

Perhaps the principal made the policy and the teacher is only following orders. Or perhaps the school board has a districtwide attendance policy. There may even be a statewide policy directing the teacher's practice. Some policies are now even imposed by the federal government, both by direct legislation and as a result of court decisions.

Therefore, a person who wishes to complain or applaud a decision or policy needs to know where it originated. If parents don't like a book their children have to read, if they don't like the cafeteria lunches or the bus schedule, they must do some research before taking action.

Build a relationship with the classroom teacher

Adults worry about textbooks, Supreme Court decisions, and administrative policies and finances. For the students, on the other hand, the success or failure of American education depends almost entirely upon who their classroom teacher is. That may sound like oversimplification of an institution as complex as the public-education system, but the more time I spend in classrooms the more convinced I am of this simple truth.

Most elementary and secondary students do not know who the superintendent of their school district is—much less the members of the school board, the state legislators, or the U.S. Secretary of Education. The students' only contact with these people and the high-level decisions they make comes through their classroom teacher. If the teacher is competent, caring, industrious, and fair, then American education is strong and sound—at least for the students under that teacher. If the teacher is insecure, overworked, short-tempered, lazy, or burned out, the system is weak and failing for that teacher's students. Education certainly needs good principals, superintendents, school boards, and sound policies; but for the student, the individual teacher is the key.

This fact should come as good news to parents who want to take an interest, and perhaps make a difference, in the way their children are educated. They need not battle a giant, impersonal system that is filled with bureaucracy and blind spots: Helping a child get a good education may be as simple as helping one teacher succeed.

Can one parent really make a difference in how any given teacher teaches? Having been a teacher, and as one who spends hours with teachers every day, I can say the answer is a resounding *yes!* Individual parents can make a great contribution to a teacher's success. Here's how:

To begin, parents should develop a personal relationship with their child's teacher. They should invite themselves to school early in the school year in order to get acquainted with the teacher. This is so important that I encourage fathers and mothers to leave work a few hours early one day, go to school, and pick up the children after class. They can use the time for a friendly conversation with the teacher in the children's presence so the kids realize the adults in their lives know one another.

Or they can invite the teacher for lunch and meet on "neutral" turf in a restaurant where both can talk more freely than in a classroom or home.

If a child is in a departmentalized school and has several teachers, the parents can simplify the process by getting acquainted with the teacher their child spends the most time with or talks about the most. If there is not enough time to meet all the teachers, a parent can develop at least one personal contact at the school. A teacher responds more positively to a child when that teacher has a positive relationship with the child's parents. The parent who has nothing specific to discuss can make a simple compliment or ask a question or pick out a lesson the child enjoyed or profited from and comment on that. Parents can help children get a better education simply by helping the classroom teacher's self-image. Any teacher who feels good about him- or herself will be a better teacher than if he or she is wallowing in a slough of self-doubt.

Develop a working relationship before problems arise

As I talk to both teachers and parents, I get the idea they do not talk to one another until a problem occurs. When that happens, the first meeting between the two sides becomes a tension-filled confrontation. Some teachers and administrators take steps to initiate communication by making phone calls and home visits in order to build relationships before problems arise.

Closing the communication gap, however, is also the responsibility of the parents. As previously suggested, they should go to the school, meet the people, and let the school personnel know they care about their child and are willing to help in whatever way they can. Two friends talking about a common problem will achieve more than two enemies battling over blame.

Think positively

With rare exception, parents and teachers want the same thing for students. Both are working to help young people through the struggles of growing up; both want children to become sensitive, moral, and responsible adults. Concerned parents should begin their interaction with the school with the belief that its people are working *with* them on a common objective.

Offer solutions

Most of us are better at finding fault than designing solutions. This is particularly true with schools. But merely pointing out flaws does not improve a situation. Finding a better way does, but it takes work.

For example, most high-school literature teachers want their students to appreciate good writing. They want them to realize that literature addresses real emotions and real feelings in such a way that a reader can understand him- or herself better.

To develop this understanding, high-school students sometimes need to read literary works about people their own age. For the past twenty years, one of the classic pieces of literature useful for this purpose has been J. D. Salinger's novel *The Catcher in the Rye*. But the book stirs controversy. It contains profanity, some bawdy scenes, and a rather negative theme. I do not like the book personally, but some high-school students have told me it is the best piece of literature they have ever read.

Suppose a well-meaning English teacher has assigned that book as required reading for my sophomore daughter. What should I do to register my opinion?

First, I should read the book. (Unfortunately, too many parents complain about books they have not read themselves, and so they have no idea exactly what is objectionable in them.)

But just reading the book is not enough. I must try to understand why the teacher has made the assignment. I need to understand the literary concept he is trying to convey with the book. (And if I don't understand, I should ask!)

Still, that is not enough if I am going to offer a positive solution. I need to know if there are other books that will convey the same concepts but without the offensive language and scenes of *The Catcher in the Rye*. I may even have to go to the library on more than a few evenings and spend time reading and evaluating books in order to develop an alternative list.

Then, when I have armed myself with that information, I am ready to go see the teacher. Now I have credibility: I know what my specific problems are with the book he has chosen; I understand what he is trying to teach; and I have some alternatives to suggest. Now I have more than a protest—I have a solution.

Teachers and administrators alike will listen to that. Even after I have done all the homework, I may not always win my case. But I have at least attracted the right kind of attention.

Making schools better is a hard job, but the work is worth it.

Consider the greater good

Public education never was and never will be value free. Every teacher makes choices and decisions that result in teaching particular values. That is inescapable. Yet the American culture, the milieu of our public schools, can be characterized by diversity, and at least one of the functions—if not the most important function—of public education in this country has always been to achieve some kind of unity within the diversity.

To accomplish this task, we sometimes must make individual sacrifices. The schools may not be able to offer all the courses my child needs to take. A new policy may be a nuisance to me but an advantage to the community as a whole. But if I am to contribute to the educational system of this country, I will understand and accept this sacrifice.

Parents tell me that they do not want their children attending school where drugs are available. Yet these same parents will protest the presence of bathroom monitors who prevent drug deals from being made in the restrooms. Parents complain about poor attendance in local schools, yet they take their children out of school without notice for family outings. Parents complain about poor test scores, yet they object to the amount of homework students are given. A school system cannot be created to accommodate just one child.

Perhaps the problems of public education may be a problem of pronouns. For all of our criticisms and conversations, most of us still look at schools as *theirs*, instead of *ours*. The failures and shortcomings of public education are *their* fault, not *ours*. The problems are *theirs* to solve, not *ours*. But until we can see American schools as ours, we will never achieve the unity of parents and educators necessary to produce the best learning climate for our young people in this era of rapid social change.

NOTES

Chapter 3. Where Have the Values Gone?

1. For a deliberate explication of cultural pluralism, see R. Freeman Butts, *The Revival of Civic Learning: A Rationale for Citizenship Education in American Schools* (Bloomington, Ind.: Phi Delta Kappa, 1980), 9–21.

2. Paul Peachey, "Toward an Understanding of the Decline of the West," *Journal of the American Scientific Affiliation* (March 1985), 29.

3. For further discussion of the response in higher education in particular, see Mark A. Noll, "The Revolution, the Enlightenment, and Christian Higher Education," in *Making Higher Education Christian*, Joel A. Carpenter and Kenneth W. Shipps, eds., (Grand Rapids, Mich.: Christian University Press, 1987), 56–76.

4. Racial injustice was a serious impediment to and an indictment of American values, but it is not being addressed because of the purpose and brevity of this chapter.

5. See Lawrence A. Cremin, *American Education: The Metropolitan Experience, 1876–1980* (New York: Harper & Row, 1988), for a scholarly discussion of Christianity and American schools.

6. A careful explanation of science and religion in historical perspective has been provided by Charles Hummel, *The Galileo Connection* (Downers Grove, Ill.: InterVarsity Press, 1986).

7. For a favorable presentation of the ideas guiding this curriculum, see Richard M. Jones, *Fantasy and Feeling in Education* (New York: New York University Press, 1968).

8. A cogent Christian perspective on these changes, particularly as manifested in the 1960s, is offered by Os Guinness, *The Dust of Death: A Critique of the Counter Culture* (Downers Grove, Ill.: InterVarsity Press, 1973).

9. Louis Raths, Merrill Harmin, and Sidney Simon, *Values and Teaching: Working with Values in the Classroom* (Columbus, Ohio: Charles E. Merrill, 1966).

10. Sidney Simon and Sally Wendkos Olds, *Helping Your Child Learn Right from Wrong: A Guide to Values Clarification* (New York: Simon and Schuster, 1976), 17.

11. For a comprehensive critique of values clarification, see Barry Chazan, *Contemporary Approaches to Moral Education* (New York: Teachers College Press, 1985), 45–67.

12. J. P. Guilford, "Three Faces of Intellect," *American Psychologist*, 14 (1959), 469–79. A quality sampling of additional readings of cognitive development is found in Richard C. Anderson and David P. Ausubel, eds., *Psychology of Cognition* (New York: Holt, Rinehart and Winston, Inc., 1965).

13. For a friendly review of Piaget and his ideas by way of interview, see *Jean Piaget: The Man and His Ideas* (New York: E. P. Dutton and Company, Inc., 1973).

14. For essays on the limitations of Kohlberg's theory from Jewish and Christian perspectives, see Donald M. Joy, ed., *Moral Development Foundations: Judeo-Christian Alternatives to Piaget/Kohlberg* (Nashville: Abingdon Press, 1983).

15. Craig Dykstra, "What Are People Like? An Alternative to Kohlberg's View," in Joy, *Moral Development Foundations*.

16. John I. Goodlad, *A Place Called School: Prospects for the Future* (New York: McGraw-Hill Book Co., 1984), 241–2.

17. Ibid.

18. Robert N. Bellah, *Habits of the Heart: Individualism and Commitment in American Life* (Berkeley, Calif.: University of California Press, 1985).

19. R. Freeman Butts, *The Revival of Civic Learning: A Rationale for Citizenship Education in American Schools* (Bloomington, Ind.: Phi Delta Kappa, 1980).

20. A constructive, Christian perspective is expounded in Mark A. Noll, Nathan O. Hatch, and George M. Marsden, *The Search for Christian America* (Westchester, Ill.: Crossway Books, 1983).

Chapter 4. The Myth of Neutrality

1. Rockne McCarthy, Donald Oppewal, Walfred Peterson, and Gordon Spykman, *Society, State, and Schools* (Grand Rapids, Mich.: Wm. B. Eerdmans Publishing Co., 1981), 90.

2. Jefferson to William Short, 31 October 1819; Paul L. Ford, ed., *Writings of Thomas Jefferson* (New York: G. P. Putnam's Sons, 1892–99), 10:144.

3. Emphasis mine; quoted in Vincent P. Lanie, *Public Money and Parochial Education: Bishop Hughes, Governor Seward, and the New York School Controversy* (Cleveland: Case Western Reserve University Press, 1968), 83. This is the earliest usage of *secular* as a synonym for *nonsectarian* of which I am aware, but it is quite possible that there are earlier instances.

4. *Committee for Public Education and Religious Liberty* v. *Regan*, 100 S.Ct. 840 (1980); *Lemon* v. *Kurtzman*, 91 S.Ct. 2125 (1971); *Aguilar* v. *Felton*, 105 S.Ct. 3232 (1985).

5. See references in Richard A. Baer, Jr., "Teaching Values in the Schools: Clarification or Indoctrination?" *Principal*, 61 (January 1982), 36.

6. Paul C. Vitz, *Censorship: Evidence of Bias in Our Children's Textbooks* (Ann Arbor, Mich.: Servant Books, 1986).

7. *United States* v. *Seeger*, 380 U.S. 163 (1965); *Welsh* v. *United States*, 398 U.S. 333 (1970).

8. Stephen Arons, *Compelling Belief: The Culture of American Schooling* (New York: New Press, McGraw-Hill Book Co., 1983), 211.

9. Copies of this paper may be obtained from the Baptist Joint Committee on Public Affairs; 200 Maryland Avenue, N.E.; Washington, D.C. 20002.

Chapter 5. The Open Door of School Reform

1. The National Commission on Excellence in Education, *A Nation at Risk: The Imperative for Education Reform* (Washington, D.C.: U.S. Government Printing Office, 1983), 5–6.

2. *A Nation Prepared: Teachers for the 21st Century* (New York: Carnegie Forum on Education and the Economy, May 1986), 57.

3. "Time for Results," (Washington, D.C.: National Governors Association, August 1986).

4. Ibid.

5. Ibid.

6. David T. Kearns and Denis Doyle, *Winning the Brain Race: A Bold Plan to Make Our Schools Competitive* (San Francisco: Institute for Contemporary Studies, 1988), 15.

7. "The People, the Press & Politics 1988" (Los Angeles: Times-Mirror, 1988).

8. *American Educator* "Statement of Principles" (Washington, D.C.: American Federation of Teachers, Volume 11, No. 2, Summer 1987), 11.

9. "The Williamsburg Charter" (Washington, D.C.: The Williamsburg Charter Foundation), adopted July 1988.

Chapter 6. A New Definition of "Public Education"

1. For a more extensive treatment of this topic, see Richard John Neuhaus, ed., *Democracy and the Renewal of Public Education* (Grand Rapids, Mich.: Wm. B. Eerdmans Publishing Co., 1987).

2. The historical material in this section is discussed in more detail in Rockne McCarthy, Donald Oppewal, Walfred Peterson, and Gordon Spykman, *Society, State, and Schools: A Case for Structural and Confessional Pluralism* (Grand Rapids, Mich.: Wm. B. Eerdmans Publishing Co., 1981); Rockne McCarthy, James Skillen, and William Harper, *Disestablishment a Second Time: Genuine Pluralism for American Schools* (Grand Rapids, Mich.: Wm. B. Eerdmans Publishing Co., 1982).

3. Prior to the 1820s, a variety of private academies, church schools, and charity schools in New York City were financed with allocations from the state's "permanent school fund." This fund was established in 1805 to support public education.

4. Bishop Hughes's evidence came from the Public School Society's 1827 Report. See Hughes, "The Petition of the Catholics of the City of New York," 21 September 1840, in *Documents of the Board of Aldermen of the City of New York*, VII, No. 40, (1840–41), reprinted in Rush Welter, ed., *American Writings on Popular Education: The Nineteenth Century* (Indianapolis: The Bobbs-Merrill Co., 1971), 104.

5. Jefferson's plan to establish a system of public elementary and secondary schools was outlined in a bill (*Bill for the More General Diffusion of Knowledge*) he presented to the Virginia legislature in 1779. For a full examination and critique of Jefferson's educational perspective, see McCarthy et al., "The Republican Vision of Thomas Jefferson," *Disestablishment a Second Time: Genuine Pluralism for American Schools* (Grand Rapids, Mich.: Wm. B. Eerdmans Publishing Co., 1982). See also David Little, "The Origins of Perplexity: Civil

Religion and Moral Belief in the Thought of Thomas Jefferson," in *American Civil Religion*, Russell E. Richey and Donald G. Jones, eds. (New York: Harper & Row, 1974), 199–200.

6. "Report of the Secretary of State upon memorials from the city of New York, respecting the distribution of the common school monies in that city, referred to him by the Senate, Document No. 86," *Documents of the Senate*, 26 April 1841, 9.

7. Ibid., 9–10; italics added.

8. Ibid., 13; italics added. At another point the secretary of state refers to the neutral or secular argument as a "sectarian principle."

9. Document No. 86, *Documents of the Senate*, 26 April 1841, 11. Spencer was critical of the Public School Society because "it provides an educational establishment, and solicits the charge of children to be placed under its exclusive control, without allowing to the parents of the pupil the direction of the course of studies, the management of the schools, or any voice in the selection of teachers; it calls for no action or co-operation on the part of these parents, other than the entire submission of their children to the government and guidance of others, probably strangers, and who are in no way accountable to these parents. Such a system is so foreign to the feelings, habits and usages of our citizens, that its failure to enlist their confidence, and induce a desire to place their children under its control, ought not to excite surprise."

10. To illustrate his proposal, the secretary of state compared a monopolistic structure for schools "to the religious establishments formed and supported by the governments of Europe, upon the plea that they are necessary to the moral instruction of the people; and that without them, their subjects would degenerate into heathenism. It was reserved for the American people to prove the fallacy of this position. An experience of fifty years has shown that religious worship has been better provided for, and attendance upon it has been more general, by being left to the free and voluntary action of the people, without the aid of any legal establishment; in other words, without any attempt to coerce the support of religious institutions, or to compel any one to participate in their advantages." *Documents of the Senate*, 18–19.

11. The "premise" is set forth by the U.S. Supreme Court in the 1963 ruling *Abington School District* v. *Schempp*.

12. William J. Bennett, *American Education: Making It Work* (Washington, D.C.: U.S. Government Printing Office, 1988), 24.

13. Ibid., 24; italics in the original.

14. Ibid.

15. Ibid., 36.

16. Consult McCarthy et al., "State and Education: European Alternatives," *Disestablishment a Second Time*; McCarthy et al., *Society, State, & Schools*, 136–44; Kenneth McRae., ed., *Consociational Democracy: Political Accommodation in Segmented Societies* (Toronto: McClelland and Stewart, 1974).

17. For a discussion of the "rights of associations," see McCarthy et al., "The Rights of Associations in American Thought and Law," *Society, State, & Schools*; McCarthy, "Liberal Democracy and the Rights of Institutions," *Pro Rege* (a faculty publication of Dordt College, Sioux Center, Iowa), June 1980; McCarthy, "Three Societal Models: A Theoretical and Historical Overview," *Pro Rege*, June 1981.

18. See, for example, Thomas James and Henry M. Levin, eds., *Comparing Public and Private Schools: Institutions and Organizations* (New York: The Falmer Press, 1988) 1:9; Henry Levin, "Education as a Public and Private Good" (Center for Educational Research at Stanford University).

19. This view of unity/diversity is set forth in "Chartered Pluralism: Reforging a Public Philosophy for Public Education" (The Williamsburg Charter Foundation).

20. Consult John E. Coons, "Making Schools Public," in Edward McGlynn Gaffney, Jr., ed., *Private Schools and the Public Good: Policy Alternatives for the Eighties* (Notre Dame, Ind.: University of Notre Dame Press, 1981); James Coleman, Thomas Hoffer, and Sally Kilgore, *Public and Private Schools* (Washington, D.C.: National Center for Education Statistics, 1981); J. S. Coleman and T. Hoffer, *Public and Private High Schools: The Impact of Communities* (New York: Basic Books, 1987).

21. Bernard Bailyn, *Education in the Forming of American Society: Needs and Opportunities of Study* (Chapel Hill: University of North Carolina Press, 1960), 11.

22. David B. Tyack, ed., *Turning Points in American Educational History* (Lexington: Xerox College Publishing, 1967), 120; Carl F.

Kaestle, *Pillars Of The Republic: Common Schools and American Society, 1780–1860* (New York: Hill and Wang, 1983), 51–52.

Chapter 10: What Is Legal? What Is Not? Religion in Public Schools

1. This answer is based on guidelines originally published by the Public Education Religion Studies Center at Wright State University.
2. *Zorach* v. *Clauson*, 343 U.S. 306, 313 (1952).
3. Ibid., 306.
4. Compare *Ill. ex rel. McCollum* v. *Board of Education*, 333 U.S. 203, 209 (1948)—in which a released-time program in which religious teachers entered public-school classrooms was held to be unconstitutional—with *Zorach* v. *Clauson*, 306, 308—in which a released-time program was held to be constitutional because, among other reasons, classes were not held on public school grounds.

SUGGESTED READING

Books

Adler, Mortimer. *The Paideia Proposal.* New York: Macmillan, 1982.

Arons, Stephen. *Compelling Belief: The Culture of American Schooling.* New York: McGraw-Hill Book Company, 1983.

Baer, Richard A., Jr. *Censorship and the Public Schools.* The First Amendment: Protecting Parents and Children from Caesar. Milwaukee: Catholic League for Religious and Civil Rights, 1985.

Berger, Peter L., and Richard John Neuhaus. *To Empower People: The Role of Mediating Structures in Public Policy.* Studies in Political and Social Processes. Washington, D.C.: American Enterprise Institute for Public Policy Research, 1977.

Blumenfeld, Samuel L. *Is Public Education Necessary?* Old Greenwich, Conn.: The Devin-Adair Company, 1981.

Boyer, Ernest. *High School.* New York: Harper & Row, 1985.

Chazan, Barry. *Contemporary Approaches to Moral Education.* New York: Teachers College Press, 1985.

Coleman, James S., and Thomas Hoffer. *Public and Private High Schools: The Impact of Communities.* New York: Basic Books, 1987.

Coons, John E., and Stephen D. Sugarman. *Education by Choice: The Case for Family Control.* Berkeley: University of California Press, 1978. With an appendix: "Introducing Family Choice in Education Through State Constitutional Change."

Cremin, Lawrence A. *American Education: The Metropolitan Experience, 1876–1980.* New York: Harper and Row, 1988.

Durkheim, Emile. *Moral Education*. New York: Free Press, 1961.

Ellul, Jacques. *The Technological Society*. New York: Alfred A. Knopf, 1965.

Gaffney, Edward McGlynn, Jr. *Private Schools and the Public Good: Policy Alternatives for the Eighties*. Notre Dame, Ind.: University of Notre Dame Press, 1981.

Glenn, Charles Leslie, Jr. *The Myth of the Common School*. Amherst: University of Massachusetts Press, 1988.

Goodlad, John. *A Place Called School*. New York: McGraw-Hill, 1984.

Healey, Robert M. *Jefferson on Religion in Public Education*. Yale Publications in Religion, 3. New Haven, Conn.: Yale University Press, 1962.

Joy, Donald M., editor. *Moral Development Foundations: Judeo-Christian Alternatives to Piaget/Kohlberg*. Nashville: Abingdon Press, 1983.

Kraft, Charles H. *Communication Theory for Christian Witness*. Nashville: Abingdon Press, 1983.

Lewis, C. S. *The Abolition of Man*. New York: Macmillan, 1978.

McCarthy, Rockne M., Donald Oppewal, Walfred Peterson, and Gordon Spykman. *Society, State, and Schools: A Case for Structural and Confessional Pluralism*. Grand Rapids, Mich.: Wm. B. Eerdmans Publishing Company, 1981.

McCarthy, Rockne M., James W. Skillen, and William A. Harper. *Disestablishment a Second Time: Genuine Pluralism for American Schools*. Grand Rapids, Mich.: Wm. B. Eerdmans Publishing Company, 1982.

Maritain, Jacques. *Education at the Crossroads*. New Haven, Conn.: Yale University Press, 1943.

Nelson, Frank. *Public Schools: An Evangelical Appraisal*. Old Tappan, N.J.: Fleming H. Revell Company, 1987.

Neuhaus, Richard John. *The Naked Public Square: Religion and Democracy in America*. Grand Rapids, Mich.: Wm. B. Eerdmans Publishing Company, 1984.

Neuhaus, Richard John, editor. *Democracy and the Renewal of Public Education*. Grand Rapids, Mich.: Wm. B. Eerdmans Publishing Company, 1987.

Rodriguez, Richard. *Hunger of Memory: The Education of Richard Rodriguez*. New York: Bantam, 1982.

Schimmels, Cliff. *Parents' Most-Asked Questions about Kids and Schools*. Wheaton, Ill.: Victor Books, 1989.

Sizer, Theodore. *Horace's Compromise*. Boston: Houghton Mifflin, 1985.

Vitz, Paul C. *Censorship: Evidence of Bias in Our Children's Textbooks*. Ann Arbor, Mich.: Servant Books, 1986.

Ward, Ted. *Values Begin at Home*. Wheaton, Ill.: Victor Books, 1989.

Worthington, Everett L., Jr. *When Someone Asks for Help: A Practical Guide for Counseling*. Downers Grove, Ill.: InterVarsity Press, 1982.

Periodicals

Phi Delta Kappan. Published by Phi Delta Kappa, Bloomington, Indiana.

Educational Leadership. Published by the Association for Supervision and Curriculum Development, Alexandria, Virginia.

ABOUT THE AUTHORS

Richard A. Baer, Jr., *is professor of resource policy and planning in the Department of Natural Resources at Cornell University and directs a program in agricultural and environmental ethics in the College of Agriculture and Life Sciences. From 1962 to 1973 he taught New Testament at Earlham College and the graduate Earlham School of Religion in Richmond, Indiana. Baer holds a doctorate in the history and philosophy of religion from Harvard University and a Bachelor of Divinity from Princeton Theological Seminary. He has done graduate study in philosophy and religion at the University of Tübingen in Germany, and he holds an undergraduate degree in philosophy from Syracuse University.*

William J. Bennett *is currently director of National Drug Control Policy. He served as United States Secretary of Education from 1985 through 1988. Prior to that, Bennett was chairman of the National Endowment for the Humanities and president of the National Humanities Center. He has a law degree from Harvard University and a doctorate in political philosophy from the University of Texas. He is the author, with Terry Eastland, of* Counting by Race: Equality from the Founding Fathers to Bakke and Weber *(Basic Books, 1979) and* Our Children and Our Country: Improving America's Schools and Affirming the Common Culture *(S&S, 1988).*

Ernest L. Boyer *is president of the Carnegie Foundation for the Advancement of Teaching and Senior Fellow at the Woodrow Wilson School, Princeton University. He is former United States Commissioner of Education and former chancellor of the State University of New York. Two major Carnegie Foundation studies,* High School *and* College, *were authored by Boyer, who also writes as the education columnist for the* London Times. *He has been named to national commissions by three Presidents and was awarded a Fulbright Fellowship in 1984.*

Samuel E. Ericsson *is executive director of the Christian Legal Society, Falls Church, Virginia. He is a graduate of the University of Southern California and Harvard Law School. Ericsson has been in the forefront of religious liberty issues, serving as general counsel to the National Released Time Religious Education Association and as counsel of record in* Bender v. Williamsport Area School District. *He is coauthor of* The Battle for Religious Liberty *(David C. Cook, 1981) and numerous other articles, and has served as an elder of Immanuel Bible Church, Springfield, Virginia.*

Charles L. Glenn *is executive director of the Office of Educational Equity, Massachusetts Department of Education, and serves as a consultant to other states and cities on issues of desegregation and parental choice. He is author of* The Myth of the Common School *(University of Massachusetts Press, 1988). Glenn has earned doctorates in education from Harvard University and in religion and modern culture from Boston University. He serves as associate pastor of an inner-city church in Boston.*

R. Lewis Hodge *is associate professor of education at the University of Tennessee–Knoxville. He earned his Ph.D. at the University of Texas, Austin. Hodge has published numerous professional papers, journal articles, and book chapters related to teacher education and value education.*

Rick Little *is founder and chairman of Quest International, a nonprofit organization based in Granville, Ohio, that develops programs for promoting positive youth development in schools and communities. Currently more than one million young people each year participate in Quest's programs in nearly thirteen thousand schools throughout the United States, Canada, and a dozen other countries. He has authored numerous articles, coauthored several books on youth issues, and appeared on television and radio programs throughout Europe, North America, Africa, and New Zealand.*

Rockne M. McCarthy *is dean of the Social Science Division at Dordt College, Sioux Center, Iowa, and an adjunct fellow of the Center for Public Justice in Washington, D.C. He has served the U.S. Department* *of Education as a review panelist on the 1985 Elementary School Recognition Program, and since 1986 on the Joint Dissemination Review Panel. He is the lead author of* Society, State, and Schools: A Case for Structural and Confessional Pluralism *(Eerdmans, 1981), and* Disestablishment a Second Time: Genuine Pluralism for American Schools *(Eerdmans, 1982).*

Cliff Schimmels *is professor of education at Wheaton College, where he has taught since 1974. Before that, he was a high school teacher and coach in Oklahoma and Texas for fifteen years. As supervisor of teaching internships, he visits about two hundred classrooms per year, and he speaks frequently to teachers, administrators, parents, and students. He has written five books about families and schools, four novels, and one book about sports.*

Ted Ward *is dean of international studies and Aldeen Professor of Missions and Christian Education at Trinity Evangelical Divinity School in Deerfield, Illinois. During his thirty years at Michigan State University, he directed the Values Development Education Center. He has served for six years as the chairman of the National Association of Evangelicals' Task Force on the Family. His research and consultation services are widely recognized among educators, and he is the author of* Values Begin at Home *(Victor, 1989).*